20 NOV 10

Dearest Lisa,

Thank you for your service to our country and your continued support to our troops.

God bless you and your family exceedingly and abundantly!

Love,

# When You've Been Broken

*A Message of God's Love, Grace & Mercy*

An Autobiography
Michelle Fernandez Cendaña

Foreword by Pastor Vera LeRay Warner

INFINITY
PUBLISHING.COM

ISBN  0-7414-5147-6

*Published by:*

**INFIN)ITY**
PUBLISHING.COM

*1094 New DeHaven Street, Suite 100
West Conshohocken, PA 19428-2713
Info@buybooksontheweb.com
www.buybooksontheweb.com
Toll-free  (877) BUY BOOK
Local Phone (610) 941-9999
Fax  (610) 941-9959*

*Printed in the United States of America*

*Published  April 2009*

# Contents

# Foreword

Some years ago, I read 'My American Journey' by Colin Powell and remember thinking the whole time I was reading his story that this man's life was pre-ordained for greatness. I was absolutely fascinated at how everything that he was presented in life was a step closer to his destiny. And I must say that I had the very same feeling while reading this book. I couldn't help but think of the Scripture in Psalm 37: 23 which states, "The steps of a good man are ordered by the Lord, and He delights in his way." None of us are here by chance and all of us were conceived in the mind of the Father before we were even born no matter the circumstances of our conception. None of us are a mistake and we were all created to worship and bring glory to God with our lives. I have heard many times the saying, "Our lives are a gift from God and what we do with our lives is our gift back to Him." Such is the life of Michelle Cendaña. Michelle chases after the heart, the will and the ways of God and I can hardly wait to see what all God is going to do with her life! She is indeed destined for greatness!

In reading her story, the reader will be drawn into how God truly does order our steps so many times through seemingly adverse circumstances to move us in the direction of destiny. Her story is one of brokenness and humility, forgiveness and how God predestines his children for purpose, and is with us every step of the way to insure that we achieve all that He has planned for our lives.

My prayer is that as you read 'When You've Been Broken,' it will cause you to reflect upon your own life and allow God to break you to make you, to order your steps and catapult you into destiny!

Vera LeRay Warner
Co-Pastor, World Harvest International Christian Center

# Acknowledgments

There are many who have had a tremendous impact in my life and contributed to the person I am today. The most important of them is my Grandmother Luisa (deceased) who lovingly raised me. To my dad, Manuel, thank you for untiringly standing by me in all my undertakings when I lived in Hawaii and when I joined the military. To my Mom Luisa, who has passed away, thank you for giving me the opportunity to come to the United States. To my sister, Lisa, and my brother, Bernie, thank you for unselfishly sharing with me your birthrights. To the Hallett Family and Ate ("Ate" means sister which is a sign of respect for a woman older than you who is not necessarily your sibling) Diana, thank you for standing by me throughout my college career. To the rest of my family and friends who watched me grow and prayed for me, my heartfelt thanks.

There were those whom God placed in my life who helped me overcome obstacles and who extended their love to me like I was one of their daughters and sisters. To Dennis and Betty Ortman, thank you for being in my life when my going was extremely tough and I was dealing with a broken heart. To Colonel (US Army Retired) Bill and Kathy Ladd, thank you for helping me build my confidence. To Denny and Jeannie, thank you for giving me words of affirmation. To Miss Millicent Guarin, thank you for your mentorship and friendship.

For those who helped me in my personal and professional military life, my sincere gratitude to the following: Colonel Robert Harms, Colonel Frederick Cross, Colonel Edwin Drose, Colonel Randall Bland, Colonel Derek and Mrs. Kristina Orndorff, Lieutenant Colonel Jarvis McCurdy, Lieutenant Colonel Jay Chapman, Lieutenant Colonel Kris Kramarich, Lieutenant Colonel Mark Rosenstein, Lieutenant Colonel Suzanne Nielsen, Major Stacy Seaworth, Major Curtis Nowak, Major Olivia Bierman, Major Joyce LuGrain,

MAJ Scott Bager, Captain Keith Cockrell, Captain Christina Fanitzi, Captain Shawn Fitzgerald, Mrs. Eunhee Dunaway, Mrs. Dolores Villanueva, Mrs. Sharyl Grimm, Mrs. Florence 'Bing' Becker, Mrs. Cathryn Campton, and William and Lauren Gonzalez.

To Pastors Michael and Vera Warner, and the members of the World Harvest International Christian Center in Nieder-Ramstadt, Germany, thank you for your love and support.

Special thanks to Captain Katherine Diefenbach and Patrick McGinley, for your friendship and for your overwhelming assistance in editing this book. To Captain Jamal Eason, thank you for your creative layout design. To Captain Paul Houk and Mr. Robert Hembrook, thank you for reviewing this book.

Above all, I thank and praise the living Lord, Jesus Christ, who gave me every reason to believe and live in God's abundant love, grace and mercy.

# Introduction

I had hesitations in sharing my life story with anyone for many years except for people I've come to know and trust. There were so many emotional challenges I had to overcome in my life that opening myself up to friends I thought might end in another episode of rejection. I always asked myself, "Will they still be friends with me if they find out who I really am?"

It took heartbrokenness for me to accept the things I denied for many years about my very existence. By the grace of God, I realized that when you've been broken, there will be a point when you begin to accept and respect the person the Lord made you to be. In disbelief, I found that when you've been broken, the Lord begins to use you for His glory, honor and praise. Further, He proves His love in ways beyond comprehension.

I lived my life as a cold and stiff person. Friends and relatives noticed that I was not an affectionate person. To not cry in public or show any weakness was a promise I made to myself. Literally, I trained myself and my heart not to show any of my vulnerabilities. However, I felt the Lord wanted me to express my affections through my life story.

For many years, I had the desire to write the story of my life, but did not know how to as I was concerned about hurting those who had been a part of my pain and suffering. At one point, I started to write my life story as fiction. Then, I thought that if I were to testify to God's love, grace and mercy, then I had to write what truly happened.

On December 17, 2006, I went to my church, the World Harvest International Christian Center, expecting the spiritual high I usually get during praise and worship. Usually, I break down and cry my heart out to Christ. This time, however, I was extremely elated that all I was doing was shouting my praises and the songs of my heart to God. At first, I looked through my purse for tissues, but couldn't find one. As we sang the second song, I said to myself, "I guess I don't need a tissue as this is a tear-free Sunday." I was wrong. We started singing the third song, "The Potter's Hand" by Hillsong Australia and my eyes started to well up with tears.

It was such an overwhelming experience I didn't understand what was going on with me. I cried aloud and ended up on my knees praying to God. I asked myself, "How lower should I get down on the floor?" Feeling weak from crying hard, I dragged myself to the back of the sanctuary where the audio-equipment sat. There Brother Perry Nibbelink saw me weeping as I walked around looking for tissues. As Brother Perry offered his tissues, I said, "I'm overwhelmed." He simply said, "Receive it."

At the back of our sanctuary, I faced the opposite of our altar still crying to God. The Lord was speaking to me in such a way that I couldn't keep up with His revelation. I said, "Lord, I need to write down what you're saying because I won't remember it all." I went back to my seat and picked up a pen and paper. I started writing and the Lord instructed me to write the story of my life and give it the title "When you've been broken." Additionally, when the Pastor was asked to pray for one of the kids involved in witchcraft, the Lord directed me to write down the passage, "Train up a child in the way he should go and when he is old he will not turn from it." After that, they took up the offering and then elder Patrick prayed, "Lord, you said to train up a child in the way he should go..." I opened my eyes and said to God, "There's no way then that the words I wrote down came from me or that I conjured up those words to write. I settled in my seat talking to the Lord and before the service ended, our pastor asked if anyone had anything to say. I couldn't help, but to speak about my encounter with the revelation of the Holy Spirit.

I came home that night in awe of God's wonders. Still trying to understand what had happened, I sat in front of my computer praying to God, "If it's really your will for me to write this book, then I pray Lord give me ideas, chapter by chapter and cover to cover. After writing three chapters on Christmas Eve, I continued to pray to the Lord as the calling came to the point of asking for strength. All the pain that I thought was forgiven and forgotten came back like it was happening again in my eyes, heart and soul. It was even more painful to relive and write in detail.

Two Sundays later, New Year's Eve service came in an unexpected way. Our pastors told us that they were led to pray for us individually at the altar. As we were being prayed for, I heard what was being said to others. I found myself pleading with God that whatever He wants to say to me on the altar, I prayed I would be able to accept it. My turn came and Pastor Vera, in a comforting soft voice said, "Michelle, the reason why you've been crying so much at church is because you've been broken." Immediately, I thought about the title of the book I was writing and it sounded like it was a confirmation to me. Then, I said to myself, "Hmmm…maybe I'm just making it up so I will wait until I get home to see if that was really the title of the book. Surely, I turned my computer on and checked the title of the book I had been working on for the past two weeks. It was "When you've been broken."

I wrote this book to share with you how the Lord worked mysteriously in each chapter of my life thus far. As you read it, my prayer is that the Lord touches your heart so that you may come to accept Him as your Lord and Savior and that you may come to accept and respect the beautiful person He created in you.

# Chapter 1

## My Childhood and Adolescence: Identity Crisis

*"Train up a child in the way he should go and when he is old he will not turn from it." Proverbs 22:6*

<u>The root of my identity crisis</u>

Constantly, I looked at myself in the mirror when I was growing up. It wasn't because I wanted to see what others saw in me, but to see what others could not see. Often, I asked myself, "Who am I? My name is Michelle Cendaña. And this is what Michelle looks like." Vividly, I remember walking away from the mirror with my questions unanswered.

Around the age of four, I began to recognize that my grandparents were not my parents. Perhaps, I wouldn't have recognized it at the time had it not been for the children in our neighborhood. My playmates bullied me and told me that I had very old parents. Although it raised my curiosity, I kept my questions to myself. There's another part of my childhood that I do not know how and when began; I used to call my Uncle Noel, daddy, and I only stopped doing so when he got married. At such a young age, I denied to accept the truth that my grandparents were not my parents. In addition, I denied accepting the truth that my biological mother died when she gave birth to me without divulging the identity of my biological father.

I thought I had a normal childhood except for the fact that my nannies or house helpers raised me because my family was always busy earning a living through their self-run business. At night, I saw my grandmother, Luisa, who would tell me bedtime stories that weren't the ordinary bedtime stories read to children today. The stories I heard from her were stories of real people she had encountered throughout her lifetime. Some stories were funny while some were depressing. At the end of all of her stories, she usually asked me what lessons I had learned from the characters in her stories. Nighttime was precious to me because Grandma and I could talk about life and my ambitions – she was my sounding board.

Despite all these lessons learned from bedtime stories, however, I was an extremely mean child especially to my nannies. I knew how to behave outside of the home so others who didn't interact with me on a daily basis had the impression that I was like an angel. Little did they know I was a 'territorial terrorist.' I clearly remember one time when I argued with my nanny and she whopped me so hard I cried and spat at her. Later, I went to her upstairs room and threw her clothes out the window. This is just one example of my most horrible behavior as a child. Since I was the only child in the house surrounded by men, I felt I always had to fend for myself and learned to be tough. The only other women in the house were my nanny and my grandma.

Love for learning

As a child, I was always eager to learn so I would tag along with my cousin, Cherry, who was one year older. She usually took me to her school where I eventually attended kindergarten and grade school. I loved to learn, but recess was a source of stress for me. At age four, when children are supposed to drink their milk from cups or glasses, I drank milk out of a baby bottle.

In the Philippines, retail stores are present on almost every corner. It's a norm to give children money so they can buy whatever snacks they want. Since I brought my baby bottle from home and did not purchase snacks or drinks from school, other children would ask me for my snack money. For no particular reason, I would give it to them. When I drank my milk, I would hide because I was embarrassed to be found drinking from a bottle since no other child did the same.

At age five, I officially attended kindergarten. I was always fascinated about learning however my mind seemed to always wonder off from the classroom. I did the best I could, but I don't think I gave all I could. I graduated from kindergarten at Salaan Elementary School, but my grandmother enrolled me in kindergarten again at a private Christian School affiliated with our church called Cinderella Kindergarten School (CKS). This was to my chagrin, but my attitude toward it quickly changed.

Cinderella Kindergarten School had so much to offer that I learned a great deal and I think it prepared me for the next grades and since I was challenged from our activities there, I gave my very best. Wholeheartedly, I did my homework the best I could. There I learned a more elaborate English vocabulary as I interacted with kids who spoke English in their households. I would say that it was at this school where I really started to learn English and the Filipino language known as Tagalog.

After attending CKS, I went back to Salaan Elementary School where almost everybody knows everybody. I had a classmate whose parents knew my family quite well and she told me that I had two fathers. As angry as I was, I couldn't do anything to prove her wrong. For some inexplicable reason, I knew that she couldn't be right, but I couldn't find proof either. Perhaps, as I looked around, no one claimed to have two fathers and one mother. For quite some time, I tried to ignore what she told me, but it never escaped my memory.

Becoming a stiff child

My family rarely talked about Minerva, my biological mother. However, at the age of seven, my family began to talk about her. I began asking simple questions about her but I can't remember my family giving me long explanations. On "All Saints Day", we would visit my mother's tomb in our town's Catholic cemetery. On her headstone, I would look at the date of her birth and her death and ask myself what my life could have been like if she were still alive.

My grandmother spoke poorly about my mother. She told me that my mother wasn't school smart and she always spent time with her friends partying. I can't remember showing any emotions toward her explanations nor was I hurt for my mother to be described that way by her own mother. Perhaps, it's because I didn't know her at all. My grandmother always encouraged me to study hard so that I would have a good future. She loved to see me studying and usually got upset if I was playing the guitar or video games.

One early sunny morning, my grandmother and I were walking side by side and she was holding my hand as we headed to our neighboring barrio. Like always, we were talking about random things. All of a sudden, she asked, "Michelle, what if I die? Who will take care of you? [Or in our vernacular she asked, "Michelle, panon to no umpatey ak. Syopatan so manasikaso ed sika?]" I don't remember crying at that point and I didn't know how to react, but I knew at that moment that I started to become a stiff child.

I always imagined myself being alone and conceived in my mind how it would be to be independent from my family members. Financially, my grandmother regularly gave me money to save, but she worried about my physical welfare. Needless to say, I was constantly planning something in my head in case my grandmother died at any time. I remember letting my imagination run wild with me living alone in a self-made hut where I was the only one who would fit. In my imagination, I would cook my own food and wash my own clothes. With those thoughts, I was scared quite often and couldn't sleep.

I wasn't an approachable person. I was always tough and because of this, I acted like one of the boys in the neighborhood. It didn't help to be surrounded by all men in the house. I preferred wearing pants and shirts than dresses

Michelle Fernandez Cendaña

and skirts. When I wore dresses, I looked twice my age because my grandmother picked them for me. When I had custom-made dresses, my grandmother picked colors that were more appropriate for older children. Needless to say, I was not a fashionable kid and I refused to follow fashion trends. That was my outward appearance and it transcended inwardly. I felt the need to be tough and matured inside and out. I didn't want to get close to anyone and thus I was not an affectionate child.

In fourth grade, our teacher asked us to stand up and tell the class what we dreamed to be when we grew up. All the other kids stood up one at a time and spelled out their goals in life. With tears in my eyes, I told the entire class that I didn't want to grow up to become like my mother and I didn't want to be a nurse. My grandmother wanted me to become a nurse like my mother. My teacher Mrs. Guadalupe Zabala, filled with compassion, told me that I had a good mother and that I would have a good future. From that point on, I promised myself to be tough and to never cry in public again.


## Competition was my watchword

My elementary school experience was filled with competitions in academics and extra-curricular activities. I joined track and field, but would always lose during intramurals. Apparently, I wasn't athletic especially because I was a scrawny malnourished-looking kid. My eating habits were poor at best because I always ate junk food and I think what saved me from getting ill was that I was extremely religious in taking multivitamins.

From first to fourth grade, I was consistently at the top of the class. I competed in everything from spelling bees to cooking contests. Some I would win and some I would lose. Whether I liked it or not, I felt that my early life's watchword was "competition."A number of my classmates' parents spread rumors that I was only at the top of the class because my grandfather used his political clout. I met the accusation with laughter and highly doubted there was truth to it.

However, my competitive edge waned in fifth grade. In class, if the lessons were too difficult or too easy, I didn't pay attention. Outside of class, I spent the majority of my time gambling with the kids in the neighborhood.

I graduated from Salaan Elementary School as the salutatorian, an accomplishment that ironically was a disappointment to my family. If I was not at the top of my class, my family felt that I didn't try hard enough. My family asked what had happened but I avoided talking about my apathy towards competition in school.

I thought competition was only happening in school, but I was wrong. At home, there was also a competition for my grandmother's love. There were periods in my childhood when my cousins moved in to my grandmother's house. One of my aunts named Natalie (name changed for the purpose of this book) hated me because my grandmother practically gave me everything. She had six children and naturally she wanted them to have my grandmother's attention, too. I am not sure if it was out of love or out of spite that she involved herself in disciplining me.

When I was misbehaving, she would spank me. I remember one time, she ran after me with a stick and I climbed a mango tree, which was in front of the house, as high as possible and stayed there for a good while. She threatened me and said she would spank me and that she was going to get a bigger stick and spank me from under the tree. When she went away, I quickly came down from the tree and headed inside the house only to find that her two older children, Ron and Jenny (names changed for the purpose of this book) were in cahoots with her and deceived me into believing their mother wasn't inside. I went inside the house and there she had a chance to whop me. That day, she accused me of being snooty to her and it was a time I'll never forget.

It seemed that my Aunt Natalie always tried to save face with my grandmother. When my grandmother was around, she was nice to me and praised me, but when Grandmother was not around, she was cruel. At times, I felt like I was in a movie and Aunt Natalie was the villain. She praised me to my face, but stabbed me when I turned around.

## The adoption process

Towards the end of 6<sup>th</sup> grade, my adoption process was finalized. My family initially talked about my possibility of living in Hawaii when I was in second grade. The legal process took a while, but my grandmother finally found an answer to her question about who was going to take care of me if she were to die. My mother's biological brother Manuel and his wife, Luisa generously adopted me. Luisa, my new Mom, would come home to the Philippines every other year and we'd spend time together with the family no matter how limited.

## Church and Sunday Schools

My grandmother may have always been busy, but she was never too busy to go to church or to check on me at church. Every Sunday, she ensured I was in church. I was practically raised in a United Methodist Church. Although churchgoing was imposed on me at such a young age, I liked going to church instead of feeling that religion was shoved down my throat. Of all the things I liked the most as a child at church was the Sunday school service. There we sang children's church songs, and listened to Bible stories. Also, I appreciated that teachers consistently prayed that God would bless me and the other children so that we may grow according to His will.

## High school life

My high school life was an adventure at Mangaldan National High School. Our school was so large, that the 5,000 students had to be divided into block sections. First year sections were named after precious gemstones, 2$^{nd}$ year's were named after wild birds, 3$^{rd}$ year's were named after flowers and fourth year's were named after Philippine heroes. In the first year, I was in the third section called Emerald.

Competition was fierce in high school and I had to study hard to be in the first section in the second year. I studied harder and my effort was not in vain. Then I found myself being in the first section called Maya and I competed quite often in oration. I spent more time memorizing speeches than studying my homework. My high school life was more of a stage performance where I learned most of my lessons superficially. While I excelled in various subjects, my grades in mathematics suffered horribly. Without exerting more effort than what was required, I convinced myself that math and I couldn't get along – I became complacent with the grades B and B+.

The second year of high school was the most memorable time in the stages of my life. I finished at the top 15 of the class but more importantly, I accepted Jesus Christ as my personal Lord and Savior. The change in me wasn't instantaneous but I praise the Lord that He is faithful in His promise to continually mold me into His image.

If you haven't received Jesus Christ in your life, I pray that as you read my salvation testimony, may you see and taste the goodness of the Lord that's manifested in a person who was a wreck like me.

### *A Renewed Life*

*I would like to share with you my old life when
I was still in control and my renewed life when I
asked Jesus to become my Lord and Savior.*

*Cheating, gambling, gossiping and disobedi-ence. These are just some of the sinful acts that I used to do that pulled me away from God. Was there a hope for a great change?*

*Through Sunday schools, I came to know Christ at a very young age. But, it didn't mean that I accepted Christ in my life. Whether or not I was willing, I had to attend Sunday church services for I was monitored by my grandmother. Going to church was an ordinary part of my life, yet my sinful ways were still so strong in me.*

*Doing good work and going to church in spite of my weaknesses were the things I trusted in for eternal life. It was not until I was a sophomore in high school that I realized I was completely wrong.*

*One Sunday morning, our Bible study group discussed salvation. Basically, it was a study on the Campus Crusades' 4 ways to live and the Inter-varsity Christian Fellowship's 2 ways to live. From the study, I learned that I was not any different from those who do not go to church. Romans 3:23 states, **"For all have sinned and fall short of the glory of God"** and **"For the wages of sin is death"** verses struck me so hard. I knew at that point that I needed Jesus Christ who died on the cross for my sins. As the discussion went along, my mathematics tutor who was our Bible study teacher asked, "If you were to die tonight and God were to ask you, why should I let you in?" Immediately, I thought of my good works, but then I realized it wasn't enough. I can't tell God the statement: One time I gave money to a beggar. I couldn't even say I was a very good person because I was a wreck. In October 1991 at age 14, I repented and accepted Christ as my Lord and Savior, for in John 14:6 it states, **"I am the way, the truth and the life. No*** *one comes to the Father except through me."* Ephesians 2:8 says, **"For by grace you have been saved, through faith- and this not from yourselves, it is the gift of God not by works, so no one can boast."** *There was no way I could go to heaven by trusting in myself and there was no way I could pay for my sins.*

*The Lord changed my life little by little. The things I liked or used to do are the things I now hate. He relieved me from my regrets and now lets me live the Christian way.*

*Christ died once and for all and by His grace He gave me eternal life. So, if I were to die tonight, I know I am saved and God will let me in to His kingdom as it is written in Ephe-sians 1:13-14* **"And you also were included in Christ when you heard the word of truth, the gospel of your salvation. Having believed you were marked in Him with a seal, the promised Holy Spirit, who is a deposit guaranteeing our inheritance until the redemption of those who are God's possession to the praise of His glory."** *He truly is the Savior.*

## Summer School at Computronix

In between my second and third year of high school, my grandmother suggested that I shouldn't waste my summer break. Although I didn't like to miss out on the school vacation fun, I enrolled in classes at a nearby computer college called Computronix to start accumulating college credits towards a computer programming degree. I learned a lot from the classes and was glad I listened to my grandmother. It was during this time that my Aunt Natalie was giving me words of encouragement that she said, "It's good that you're taking computer programming. When you get to Hawaii, you'll have a good job." For a second, I almost appreciated her. In reality, behind my back, my aunt mocked me among my relatives with remarks such as: "Let's see if Michelle graduates from college and let's see if she even gets to Hawaii."

In my third year of high school, I focused on winning competitions. From oratorical competitions to Science Investigatory Project competitions, I tried everything. Similar to elementary school, winning was the goal, but I wasn't always successful. When I won, I felt my efforts were not in vain and I was happy, but when I lost I never was gracious to myself.

The summer break between my third and fourth year went to waste. My grandmother once again encouraged me to continue taking classes at Computronix, but I insisted I needed a break. What I didn't tell her was that I wanted to do what other schoolmates were doing which was taking a break and enjoying reading romance novels. By the end of our break, I felt I wasted time and wished I went to school for the summer as the books I read were far from productive and irrelevant to my preparation for the upcoming and final year of high school.

There were many challenges for me in my fourth year at high school and one of them was relational. My classmates and other schoolmates labeled me as one of the most arrogant students. As harsh as it sounded, I began to ask God to humble me. At first, I thought that they confused confidence with arrogance particularly because they saw me on stage performing quite regularly. But honestly, people sensed characteristics of my personality that I did not recognize in myself at that time.

During my high school graduation rehearsals, I spoke with a few of my schoolmates about my personality. One of them was a person who used to look at me in either disgust or disdain, who out of nowhere asked me to sign her autograph page of her yearbook . Truthfully, I didn't like her for that throughout our time in high school, however, my Aunt Debbie convinced me to pray for her so that the Lord would bless her. I felt that the words of my Aunt Debbie was right.

Leaving for Hawaii

Since the second grade when my family talked about going to the US and living in Hawaii, I always dreamed about the US. Ten years after the initial family discussion about the US, the dream finally became a reality. In preparation for my move to Hawaii, I had to collect a series of legal documents. During my research, I uncovered some significant details about the death of my biological mother. Comparing my birth certificate to my mother's death certificate, I learned that my mother was pronounced dead only six hours after she gave birth to me. I was shocked–I was born at 5:30 am and she died at 11:30am. Despite learning this fact about my past, I was still excited to go to Hawaii.

To finalize my US immigrant visa process, my mom, sister and I went to the United States Embassy in the capital city of the Philippines for a personal interview. When we got there, the line to enter the building wrapped around the block. Luckily, Lisa, my sister, and my mom were already US citizens and we were able to skip to the front of the line. Once inside, the interview process didn't go as smoothly as I anticipated. Even though I had all the required documents to apply, my interviewer was rude to me and my family. At that time, the interviewer told me that in the case that I find other biological relatives, I would not be able to bring them to the US. Lisa, in her typical assertive manner, interjected in the interview on my behalf and essentially said that I was a part the family. With that assertion from my sister, the officer quickly stamped my visa form, handed it back to me, and directed me to go to another booth to pay the $200.00 processing fee.

After getting my visa, everything happened quickly. My mom's flight back to Hawaii was in two days. At that time, I had no clothes and I still hadn't said goodbye to my grandmother who was in Pangasinan (a province that is about 233 kilometers north of Manila). Fortunately, my Uncle Wilson went back to the province to fetch my grandmother and to get my clothes. When my grandmother arrived, she bought me clothes and purchased my plane ticket to Hawaii. I was so thankful that my grandmother was so generous and that I was able to say goodbye to her before I left to Hawaii.

To accompany me on my flight to Hawaii, my mom arranged for me to fly with Uncle Mario. The challenge was to meet Uncle Mario, whom I've never met, at the departure gate. I was afraid we were not going to recognize each other. The adventure to meet my uncle at the airport terminal began at the immigration/passport control point. Like most foreign travelers to the US, I lugged around a huge clear bag containing all my medical paperwork; a sure sign that I was on my way to the US. There was an airport attendant who saw me walking alone with my clear bag that asked me who sponsored me to go to the US. When I told her that it was the relatives who adopted me she replied, "You're very lucky." When I finally got to the departure gate, I found my uncle. Uncle Mario was such a comedian that not only was it easy for me to recognize him, but we both got along great. Undoubtedly, I counted myself blessed.

# Chapter 2

## Hawaii: Going Through the Refiner's Fire in "Paradise"

*"...because the Lord disciplines those he loves, and he punishes everyone he accepts as a son." Hebrews 12:6*

Arriving in the Hawaiian fleet of islands, I was in awe of its beauty as the plane was descending on to the Island of Oahu. From above, I admired the crystal blue and green waters of the Pacific Ocean that surrounded the islands. At last, I arrived in what many describe as paradise. My Mom met me at the Honolulu International Airport on the island of Oahu with a nice, fresh lei. I still can picture how I looked: sporting short hair, wearing jeans and a white long sleeved shirt and a pair of Nike basketball shoes that Mom bought me. With a lei around my neck, security personnel by the carry-on X-ray scanners knew I was new to Hawaii. They smiled and greeted me with a warm "Aloha."

The first three weeks on Maui was all about watching television, attending family gatherings and applying for a job. Boredom set in. I told my dad I really wanted to start working. My dad said, "You need to enjoy the time you aren't working for once you start, you'll barely have a break." Still, I wanted to work and to not just lounge around. My Aunt Salome accompanied me to apply for a job at McDonald's. Immediately, I was hired and could start work at any time. In my mind, working at McDonald's was a good start especially since I just arrived in the US.

Working at McDonald's helped me understand what hard work means. My schedule was from 5:00am to 1:00pm. I worked long and hard on the grill in the kitchen flipping bacon, buns and burgers. I soon realized how hard it was to earn money. All my life I thought it was easy to make money so I had always asked my grandparents for money as if it grew on trees. The first time I received my pay check for $48, I didn't want to cash it in nor did I want to spend it on the frivolous things I used to buy – I wanted to frame it.

## Beginning of my struggles

The early shift at my McDonald's job began to create scheduling problems in the family due to our limited transportation options. Consequently, I quit my job to pursue other work options that would fit the family's schedule. After a week of searching, I was unable to find another job. The job rejections bruised my confidence however, I didn't let the process discourage me. Fortunately, on my last day of job searching for the week in which I had planned to return my McDonald's uniforms, my former boss asked me to come back to McDonald's. She had received numerous compliments about my customer service performance and wanted me back on the McDonald's team. With the help of my father, my boss and I negotiated a better work schedule and I returned to work the following day. I thanked God for His blessings and allowing me to stay employed.

In the free time between my off hours at McDonald's, I took a part-time job at Foodland Supermarket. The manager told me that I couldn't be a cashier since they were selling alcoholic beverages and I was still under the legal drinking age. I gladly took a job there as a courtesy clerk which entailed bagging groceries, mopping the floor and whatever else was needed for the upkeep of the store.

At 18, I was working at least 14 hours a day. I have no doubt that work helped me keep my sanity and it helped me continue to dream for a better future. One of my dreams was to finish college. An opportunity came where I enrolled in a computer class which was sponsored by Maui Community College. That was my first exposure to

American education. I thanked my cousin, Sherwin, who accompanied me to sign up for the class. I enjoyed it and learned a lot. At that point, I wished and hoped that I could go back to college full time.

Outside of work, I had the responsibility to help out my family. At times, going to school, working at McDonald's, the supermarket and helping everyone else felt like three full time jobs. My life practically revolved around work and home and I had no friends outside of work. Every day, I tried my best to please my family but sometimes I felt my best was not good enough. I began to long for my life in the Philippines in which I had more free time and social life. After six months of balancing the demanding schedule and responsibilities in the Hawaiian "paradise", I told my dad that I wanted to go back to the Philippines.

My dad did not really like the idea that I wanted to go back to the Philippines. He wanted me to prosper in life and he thought that by going back to the Philippines would not be the best solution to my problems. I still had the one-way ticket to San Francisco, which my grandmother had paid for in order for me to get to Hawaii from the Philippines. Perhaps, going to San Francisco was a good idea. However, it didn't feel right for me to inconvenience our relatives there and I had no idea what I would do in San Francisco. Or as another possibility in order to find balance in my life, I could go back to the Philippines and help out in my grandmother's business while attending college ---I didn't know what to do.

The longer I stayed in Maui, the more I longed to go back to the Philippines. I literally lived in the confines of my room. Once I completed my chores, I occupied myself by reading books and listening to Christian music and radio programs. This was the time I felt the closest to God in my life. I developed a stronger trust with the Lord and found that I could depend on Him to meet my every need. I soon relied on Him to make it through each day with a positive outlook.

# Chapter 3

## The US Army: An Escape from "Paradise"

*"No temptation has seized you except what is common to man. And God is faithful; he will not let you be tempted beyond what you can bear. But when you are tempted, he will also provide a way out so that you can stand up under it." 1 Corinthians 10:13*

<u>Appointment with an Army recruiter</u>

One ordinary morning, my sister asked me to accompany her to an appointment in Wailuku, Maui's business district which is a 45 minute drive from Lahaina. Since I was scheduled to work at my part time job, I told her that I couldn't go with her. She promised that I would be at work on time. Without telling me where she had an appointment, I went with her. As we pulled in to a fenced in compound, I read "US Army Recruiting Station Maui" in bold letters at the facade of the building. Uncertain of what to think about what I just read, I was nervous beyond reason and wondered what we were about to do there. In addition, I remembered what my uncle told me before I left the Philippines. Out of nowhere, my uncle said, "I hope you don't join the US Army when you get to Hawaii."

We walked in to the building and were greeted by a Japanese-Hawaiian looking Army recruiter, Sergeant First Class (SFC) Takushi. Still in disbelief that we were in a military recruiting station, I looked around the office while my sister was guided to a computer booth to input her information. There were so many racks of Army pamphlets in front of me, I was overwhelmed and fearful of even learning about the military. Moments later after speaking with my sister, the recruiter asked if I also wanted to join the military. Without hesitation, I told him no. I told him about the horrifying newspaper articles I had read on women getting raped and abused in the military---situations that I didn't want to be exposed to. SFC Takushi didn't deny that situations like that happen in the military, but he assured me that there are precautions they take in order to prevent situations like that from happening and that they have strict laws.

SFC Takushi persistently suggested that I take the Armed Service Vocational Aptitude Battery (ASVAB) test and stated that if I passed it wouldn't mean that I would join the Army. When my sister finally finished the process of inputting her information at the computer booth, SFC Takushi mentioned that study guides were available at the public libraries. Further, he said that if we were ready, the test would be administered the following Thursday. Keeping her promise, my sister dropped me off at my part time job after we picked up study guides from the Lahaina Public Library.

## From benchmark test to physical exam

Sacrificially, I studied during my breaks at work which were essentially in increments of 30 minutes, but it was better than not studying at all. Since I was working 14 hours a day, my sister and I almost never had a chance to study together. When we did, however, it was only briefly since I would come home from work at almost midnight. A week passed and it was time to take the test on Thursday. I thought I did a decent job on the exam, but I didn't think I did well enough to pass it because I was reading and answering the questions so slowly that I didn't answer all the questions on the test.

Three days after we took the test, my sister was on the phone with the recruiter who told her that I passed the

Michelle Fernandez Cendaña

test. I was ecstatic in knowing that my brain still functioned despite being out of school full time for nearly a year by that time. The recruiter told me that if I took the physical exam and passed it, it wouldn't mean I would join the Army. I subjected myself to the Army physical exam in Honolulu on the island of Oahu. Amazingly, I flew in and had a chance to bask in the busy streets of Waikiki on the island of Oahu and stayed in a nice hotel. I never thought Army trainees would be treated nicely with hotel accommodation during the in-process. The physical exam was a one day process. I flew back to Maui with the intent to pursue the Army application process, but my decision-making proved to be a difficult one.

The physical exam result came back with a slight problem. At 102 pounds I barely made the weight standard for entrance into the US Army. Moreover, I had to be evaluated for my allergies. The military doctors explained to me that I would need a medical waiver for my allergies in order to be admitted into the military. This was about the time when I called upon the Lord asking if the Army was for me. After several visits to the Army hospital I received my medical waiver and I knew that the Lord had intervened. SFC Takushi was extremely helpful in this process as he not only picked me up and dropped me off at the airport, but he was also a source of encouragement.

SFC Takushi informed me that my allergy waiver request was approved. He then asked to see me so we could talk about what jobs were available for me. In the Army I wanted a job that had something to do with computers. SFC Takushi had me read through various job descriptions and I thought Automated Logistics Specialist was the best job for me. SFC Takushi asked when I would like to leave for training. Anxious to start the next chapter of my life, I told him to send me as early as possible. Consequently, he scheduled me to leave in three months. Nothing was going to hold me back from joining the Army

To transition into the Army, I first had to submit my resignation at my full-time jobs. Secondly, about one month before my Basic Combat Training, I resigned from my part-time job.  The evening of my resignation from my part-time job, I told everyone at home of my decision and that I needed to prepare physically for about a month.  At the time, I was not very athletic. To prepare for basic training, I had a daily regimen of push-ups and sit-ups and running to get myself in shape.

The day before I left for basic combat training, my family threw a farewell party for me at Auntie Belen's house.  They all seemed to be so happy for me.  On November 1, SFC Takushi picked me up from my house to drop me off at Kahului Airport on the island of Maui.  I then spent one more day on the island of Oahu in Honolulu. There I signed my contract, sworn to defend the United States and its Constitution and then headed off to Fort Leonard Wood, Missouri for my Basic Combat Training.

# Chapter 4

## Basic Combat Training: Carrying Excess Baggage

*"Take my yoke upon you and learn from me, for I am gentle
and humble in heart, and you will find rest for your souls.
For my yoke is easy and my burden is light." Matthew
11:29-30*

Basic Combat Training

      Before departure at the Honolulu MEPS (Military
Entry Processing Station), all of us trainees were briefed
about what we could and could not do now that we were
bound by the Uniform Code of Military Justice (UCMJ). Of
all the things they told us, what stuck in my memory was to
not harass flight attendants. They gave us all sorts of
paperwork to include our plane tickets. I was instructed that
I was in charge of one male trainee who was heading to the
same training I was attending until we in-processed at Fort
Leonard Wood, Missouri.

      The plane touched down at Saint Louis International
Airport late morning. I can't remember the temperature, but
it was freezing. There was a slight delay for us unboarding
the plane and I could remember sitting still in my seat with
my chattering teeth. I was wearing a light coat appropriate
for an island's extreme weather condition, but not for a cold
winter environment. Once we got off the plane, I called
home just to let my family know that I made it safely.
Afterwards, we waited for our two-hour bus ride to Fort
Leonard Wood at the USO (United Services Organization)
lounge at the airport.

Once the trainees and I arrived at Fort Leonard Wood, we began our in-processing to our new military unit. The first step was to throw away all contraband items in our possession in order to focus on our military training. Our military cadre ordered us to rummage through our belongings to remove all food, over-the-counter medications and weapons. Over the next three-days, we were issued military uniforms, got haircuts and received presentations on how to be a soldier.

During the in-processing phase, all the new trainees marched from one location to another. One morning, when we marched to pick up our uniforms, it started to snow. It was my first time seeing snow and in fascination, I observed snowflakes falling to the ground and almost forgot where I was.

On the fourth day, we reported to our training company. We rode cattle trucks in full uniform with all our personal belongings and issued equipment. Once the trucks arrived outside of our military dormitories (barracks), the drill sergeants began to scream at us to get off the trucks. While some of the trainees were laughing and having a good time, I was scared and nervous. Thankfully, I kept my composure. Those who didn't were ordered by the drill sergeants to do push-ups and other exercises until the trainees felt that their arms were going to fall off .

Basic Combat Training wasn't easy for me. There were things I had to face such as understanding military lingo, overcoming cultural barriers, and building my muscular endurance. With different accents of drill sergeants and fellow trainees, I had to read people's lips and listen to them intently just to keep up. In reflection, I remember a humorous incident with a drill sergeant, in which he ordered me to stack milk crates in a storage room. As if he had a severe nasal congestion, he yelled, "Private, stack them side by side. Do you speak another language?" Without hesitation, I said ,"Yes, drill sergeant." He shook his head in disgust and left me alone. Lastly, on top of all of these adjustments, I frequently thought about Hawaii and my role that I use to have at home.

The first week of training, I followed the new trainee crowd so often that it led me to trouble. One time during lunch, I had left the cafeteria lunch line and was heading towards the seating area. A group of trainees were heading towards an empty table. Unknowingly, I followed; a mistake that I won't forget. When the trail of trainees was almost to the table, we passed the drill sergeants eating area. This was unacceptable to the drill sergeants and they made us yell at the top of our lungs, "I will not disturb the drill sergeants' lunch." After that incident I thought I was done. However, as I completed my meal and was about to return my tray, one of my fellow trainees offered to take the tray for me. Instead of letting him take my tray, I quietly told him that it was taken care of. From across the room, the eagle of the drill sergeant saw that my mouth was moving---I was in trouble again. Again, I had to yell, "I will not talk in the dining facility" until my voice was gone. Ironically, during the initial evaluation period, the drill sergeants noted that I had a high adaptedness towards military lifestyle.

For a brief period at basic training, I made more enemies than friends. Fellow trainees created cliques and if a person was not in their group, they were an outcast. There were a few good friends to include Tulai Fata from American Samoa, Libby Gregory from Nevada and Liz Cromer from California who all helped me get through basic training.

The third week of the training was focused on Rifle Marksmanship. To get ready for training, we would wake up at 0430 in the morning. One of the drill sergeants who was not our assigned drill sergeant complemented my shots at the ranges. He told me that I could be a sniper. I laughed because I didn't like shooting and the first night I was handed a weapon I shed tears because carrying a weapon was not something I imagined myself doing. The week went on and we kept on qualifying in a number of ranges. Oddly, I always qualified except during qualification day. With three attempts I was unable to successfully complete a range qualification during our field training exercise. My failure reminded me of previous failures; I felt depressed and unsure if I could even make it through basic training.

## Christmas vacation in Illinois

Christmas holiday came and it meant all trainees were allowed to go on 'exodus leave' for two weeks. Deciding to go home was stressful for me. I didn't know if I wanted to fly all the way back to Hawaii to dive back into my previous home life. Thankfully, I had an alternative. My cousin Liela gave me her sister Sarah's phone number who lived in Naperville (a suburb of Chicago), Illinois. I called Ate Sarah to ask if I could stay with her. The plane ticket only cost $99 to Illinois while the ticket to Hawaii cost $750. When I purchased my ticket, I called home to let my family know that I was going to Illinois for my leave.

Despite the fact that I only saw Ate Sarah once in Hawaii while she and her family were on vacation I decided to spend Christmas with her and her family. Leaving all Army uniforms behind at Fort Leonard Wood, Missouri, I collected the clothes I brought with me from Hawaii to wear while in Illinois.

From St. Louis, Missouri, I boarded the plane for Chicago. The 49-minute flight was extremely short and interesting as the man sitting next to me conversed with me about his father's service in the military. It was very interesting as I counted myself lucky to be in conversation with a random person, but who inspired me with his own life stories. He graduated from Harvard University and thought about joining the service, but he had a medical condition that precluded him from entering the military. In awe, I thanked him for sharing his stories with me.

Arriving at Chicago O'Hare International Airport in my Class A (Green suit-like uniform) and black trench coat, I wondered if my cousin's husband Kuya (a Filipino term of respect for older brother) Mason would recognize me. As I waited at the arrival area, a Caucasian man, who looked like a business man, asked me where I was headed. After I told him, he carried on a conversation with me and later asked if I would be willing to quickly watch his luggage while he went to the bathroom. Willingly, I watched his belongings, but when he returned, I asked how he could trust me without knowing me. He said, "I knew I could trust you because of the uniform you're wearing." Surprised, I quickly realized that the uniform I was wearing was a symbol of a time-tested culture and tradition of selfless service to the United States and the American people. The man thanked me and picked up his luggage and went to meet his party that fetched him from the airport. A little later, Kuya Mason and his son picked me up.

It was already dark and dreary and the 30-minute drive from the airport to Naperville seemed to be endless. When we arrived at my cousin's house, Ate Sarah was extremely elated telling me that she rarely had family members come to visit and that she was happy to have me over the holidays. Gladness overcame me in knowing that her entire family welcomed me into their home. There were great memories I had in Illinois. They took me to Chicago and I was humbled to see the skyline of the windy city. The city was absolutely beautiful and captivating that I told myself that there were definitely more interesting places outside of Hawaii. While in Chicago, my cousins and I went to museums and large malls.

In Naperville, I had a chance to play in the snow and take pictures. I savored every minute of being out in the cold and admired the mounds of snow on the ground and the pretty formation of icicles in the trees. A number of times, I got to enjoy running outside on icy roads. Like a child who was new to winter, I didn't care how dreary and cold it was outside. All I wanted to do was to have fun and for the first time, I forgot all about the rigors of basic combat training.

The Lord showed me how to feel loved in Illinois. From Ate Sarah to her in-laws, they showed how much they cared about me and told me that they love me. I was shocked to have met affectionate people for I had only experienced love implied and not expressed. Truly, I admired my cousin's family values which operated in love and harmony.

Two weeks quickly passed by and I was heading back to the reality of training when I realized that I no longer had difficulty gaining weight. While on leave, I gained seven pounds to my gladness. I was no longer skin and bones that the wind carried away in the direction it blew. It was about this time when I realized that the time came for me to seriously study the "Common Tasks Skills." About a week before I returned from leave, I studied long and hard only to find that I had more time than I ever gauged. My drill sergeants decided that I needed to transfer to another company to be retrained in rifle marksmanship.

Upon my return to Fort Leonard Wood, my world seemed to collapse in around me. Imagine finishing the first six weeks of intensive military basic training only to be placed back to the third week. One Sunday morning at church, I poured my heart out to Christ wondering why He was allowing me to go through more hardships. The days were long when we were placed on details as we waited for our new training schedule. We were stuck answering phones, shoveling snow, and organizing supply rooms. Negativity occupied my mind on a number of occasions. I asked myself what I would do in case I failed basic training.

Going back home was not an option. I called home and told my family about what happened. My mom seemed to understand and she told me that if I didn't make it, I could go home and work and go back to school. Deliberately, I planned on asking Ate Sarah if she would take me in until I could stand on my feet. I called Ate Sarah and Ate Salome crying. They both comforted me with words of affirmation. Unexpectedly, one dreary afternoon, our company executive officer named First Lieutenant Willard noticed how sad I was. He asked me why I looked sad. When I told him of the situation, he replied, "Don't worry. You'll be a highly trained private." As simple as those words sounded, it encouraged me.

Meanwhile, the rest of our fellow trainees from our old platoon took their physical fitness test. A number of them failed. One of them went AWOL (Absent without Leave) for she couldn't bear the fact that she failed her fitness test, but turned up two days later. Although I was removed from our old platoon, a few of my fellow trainees updated me of the platoon's situation when they saw me on detail. Not long after making amends and friends with our old platoon, I was transferred to another company.

With open arms, the trainees in the new company welcomed me. The drill sergeants were nice to me. They made me one of their administrative secretaries after they found out that I had completed my first year of college. The training was still grueling, but it became bearable for I already knew what to expect. Marksmanship qualification came and I shot sharpshooter. Physical Fitness test came and praise the Lord I didn't have trouble qualifying. After the field training, I knew I was well on my way to graduating.

Our graduation was held in a movie theater. The ceremony began with the playing of the national anthem and the American flag was swaying freely on the widescreen. Although excitement and gladness were in my heart since I was almost was done with basic training, I felt horrible thinking that I'd turned my back on the Philippines. I always knew in my heart that I was not a patriotic Filipino, but after learning about the Philippine Constitution, I sensed that somehow I was proud of my heritage and rights. After the ceremony, we went back to our barracks and were given a chance to call home. On the phone, I cried to my dad as I felt I was a traitor. My dad consoled me and said, "Michelle, if you feel that bad, then think of it as a job…that the US Army hired you." I guess that's another way to look at the situation I thought. The next day, after graduation, we flew flew to Virginia for Advanced Individual Training (AIT) at Fort Lee (the Army's School of Logistics).

# Advanced Individual Training

Departing through a familiar airport, Chicago O'Hare International, I mailed post cards and proceeded to the gate of departure. Although I didn't know what to expect at AIT, I wondered what the training would be like while on the plane and I was grateful at the same time that basic training was behind me--- or so I thought. I arrived at Richmond in the afternoon, but we didn't get picked up from the airport to Fort Lee until late evening. Once we got off the bus at Reception, it felt like basic training all over again. Drill Sergeants were screaming at us and the total "shake down" (or inspection) of our belongings seemed forever. When we finally got to bed it was past midnight. I was exhausted but I knew I had to wake up at 4:30am the next morning to take a physical fitness test. The next morning I was still jetlagged, but I gave 110% physical effort to pass the fitness test so that I could ensure that I could get a seat in the class. Praise the Lord it was over and we were on our way to W Company.

The day we boarded the bus to get to W Company from the in-processing center, I never forgot the sight of our drill sergeant for the next four months. He was short, but looked mean and could pass for a Filipino or Korean. The second we got off the bus, he yelled at us and had us doing push-ups, sit-ups and running-in-place. Most of the traumatic events I've chosen to forget, but his comments are still vivid memories. When my hair fell out of the bun he said, "Private Cendaña, either fix your hair or cut it." Well, that was simple; I cut it off. There was a point when I asked myself if the drill sergeant was tough on me because I was Filipino like himself, but I talked myself out of that ridiculous thought. A few weeks into our training, the drill sergeant started to talk with me a little bit more. One afternoon, he casually asked me questions while I was standing at parade rest (standing with hands placed behind my lower back and my feet shoulder width apart). Apparently, he read through my personal data which indicated that I was born in the city of Dagupan in the Philippines.

He asked me if I lived in Dagupan. Frankly, I told him that I was just born in a hospital in that city, but I lived in a town called Mangaldan. Furthermore, he took an interest in my middle name which in the Filipino tradition, is supposed to be my mother's maiden name. He was wondering if I was related to any Fernandez from Dagupan City. Although it may have been the case, it would be needle-in-a-haystack to point out who were my relatives. Suddenly, he said, "My ex-fiancée married a Fernandez and she didn't even give me back my ring." No words slipped my mouth, but my brain processed words that weren't verbalized 'Your problem has nothing to do with me.'

Two and a half months of training in St. Petersburg, Virginia was bearable. The first half of the day was spent in the classroom while the other was utilized for training and study halls. As days went by, I met with upper classmen and asked them what I should do in order to finish successfully and with honors. They told me to study hard and continue to be disciplined like a soldier. Clearly, I remember asking soldiers on duty at night (whom we call Fire Guards) to wake me up in the middle of the night so I could study. Only the bathroom light was left on all night. When the fire guards woke me in the middle of the night, I went to the bathroom with my notes and studied.

There were a number of inspections where drill sergeants had trainees stand next to their wall lockers while the drill sergeants checked for neatness and prohibited paraphernalia. Inspections were also an opportunity for drill sergeants to ask military knowledge. One cloudy afternoon, an inspection was conducted by the senior drill sergeant. She drilled my brain with question after question. Later, she told me that I needed to appear before the soldier of the Month Board. I was perplexed, because the drill sergeant had already selected our class representative for the company competition. The senior drill sergeant told the drill sergeant that based on the result of her inspection, I was the best candidate.

Ecstatic and nervous at the same time, I only had a few days to study in addition to our daily school require-ments. To my delight, I attributed everything to God's grace that I won the competition. I could not wait to share the news with my family and friends. The following day, however, I got scolded by our First Sergeant when she woke us all up around 4:30am to conduct inspection. My wall locker was anything but organized. Out of her frustration, she said, "I'm disappointed soldier. Your senior drill sergeant said you're the best soldier in your class, but look at your locker." I took what she said to heart and no one ever found my locker disorganized again.

All the late nights, hard work and discipline paid a huge dividend at the end of AIT. To my drill sergeant's surprise, I graduated with honors. In my mind, I accom-plished my goal. During the graduation ceremony, I remember feeling extremely happy. As I walked off the auditorium stage, my First Sergeant who stood by the stairs to shake my hand said, "You made it, skinny." I thanked her and laughed in disbelief about what she had just called me. She stated what was obvious, but I felt that I no longer fit the "skinny" category for I had gained weight since joining the Army.

Training was over and I was ready to tuck away the great memories I had with our instructors and classmates or co-trainees. I couldn't wait to get to my first duty station to apply what I had learned, but more importantly, to get away from the sight of drill sergeants. Unfortunately, there was one more training, a functional course (or what we call "additional skill identifier") that kept me at Ft. Lee for another two weeks.

Michelle Fernandez Cendaña

# Functional Course

Only a few days after graduation from AIT, I, along with another classmate, moved to I Company (a company for "permanent party" or prior service soldiers who are reclassifying from their current MOS). Wondering how we were picked for the additional course, we were told that we were randomly selected. My hope to stay away from drill sergeants did not come quickly, but at least in this company they were a little bit more lenient. Our barracks were the same as the ones I stayed in before at AIT, but they had larger bays.

Another good thing I noticed was that we could eat at any dining facility we wanted except where there were AIT students. I was in such a training mode that I barely understood the difference. Since I didn't have a car, I walked with friends to dining facilities or sometimes friends offered me rides. One morning, I went to the Army and Marine dining hall and was surprised to be spotted by a family friend named Reggie from the Philippines and Hawaii. From a distance, I heard my name called and when I looked, I was elated because there was no way I would have recognized him if he didn't see me first because of his hair cut; his hair was nearly shaved off.

All of us in I Company had different schedules of classes except for physical fitness where we ran as a group nearly every day. Our classroom instructors were also more lenient since they were teaching those who had been in the Army more than a day. Our class was so small we got to know each other quickly. We had classmates who were senior Non-Commissioned Officers. In this company, I tasted what it would be like at a Regular Army duty station. We dined with our classmates in an outside civilian restaurant for the sake of camaraderie. The days flew quickly by and before I knew it, I was on my way to Germany---my first duty station.

The day before I left for Germany, me and the other trainees had to work outside to beautify the military post. We were working in the midday sun and I was getting dehydrated which my drill sergeant noticed. Later, the drill sergeant sent me packing to get ready for my flight. I took a cab to Washington Dulles International Airport in order to take a military chartered flight. The entire time I longed for a refreshing glass of water to quench my thirst. However, I had too many things to do to get on my flight I had to delay getting water.

I clearly remember the briefing I received at the Honolulu Military Entry Processing Station on how to properly interact with flight attendants. After the aircraft went airborne and the flight attendants started to serve meals, I thought it was my chance to ask for water. A flight attendant walked by and I asked for water, his reply was "I don't have water in my hand." I was speechless; I thought his comment was uncalled for. For what seemed to have been forever, I replayed his response in my head many times, I could not believe the attendant's response to my simple request. As silly as it may sound, I let it pass. Surprisingly, he came back with a glass of water nearly half an hour later. A little later, an attendant was serving water so I asked for another glass. The same attendant was right behind her and in passing he smartly remarked, "I guess somebody is hydrating;" a comment obviously referring to me. Again, I didn't say a word to express my disgust of his impolite comment.

# Chapter 5

## First Duty Station: God's Deliverance and Healing

*"Because he loves me," says the Lord, "I will rescue him; I will protect him, for he acknowledges my name. He will call upon me, and I will answer him; I will be with him in trouble, I will deliver him and honor him." Psalm 91:14-15*

<u>In-processing at Rhein Main Airbase</u>

The aircraft landed at Frankfurt International Airport before lunch time on a warm July morning in 1996. Military liaisons at the Rhein Main Airbase gathered all of us who were on a permanent change of duty station to Germany and gave us a briefing. Although jetlagged, I was well aware of the contents of my bags. I had three days' supply of civilian clothing and my military issued uniforms. Afraid that there would be another "shake down" of my belongings for restricted food items, I quickly rummaged through my carry on and took out my favorite junk food--- honey-mustard pretzels. After disposing the pretzels, I looked around me and realized that I was the only one throwing away "contraband." A few minutes later, they took us to 1st Replacement Company for in-processing.

At 1st Replacement, there were two type of soldiers: those that had assignments and those who did not. Without an assignment, soldiers would have to wait around for days for an organization to request their specific job specialty. Fortunately, I had an assignment to Augsburg, Germany and expected to be picked up by my unit by the end of the day. While we waited, the 1st Replacement military cadre, allowed the new soldiers to go to the dining hall to eat lunch.

I remember enjoying my meal as I conversed with two other soldiers who were also headed towards Ausburg.

After eating lunch, I boarded the bus to Augsburg. I was surprised to see that there were only three people aboard the bus. In preparation for the bus ride that I thought was going to be four hours, I pulled out my German phrase book, my travel pillow and my bottle of water and got myself comfortable for the long ride. However, only ten minutes into the trip, the bus driver abruptly stopped the bus and pulled over to the side of the road, and yelled back to the passengers in broken English "Get off the bus!" I didn't know what was happening, did I do something wrong? With a flashback memory of my anti-terrorism briefings, perhaps we were under a terrorist attack. I didn't know; I panicked. But I packed my belongings up in my bag as instructed. Once off the bus, I noticed a small van parked on the side of the road. The driver explained that with only three people, a van can get us to Augsburg. What a relief, at least I was not in trouble, and in a few minutes we were on our way.

Although the road trip took four hours, I didn't sleep. I was looking at the countryside and kept attempting to learn to pronounce German words from my German phrase book which was a gift from Ate Sarah's neighbor and friend, Becky. The countryside sceneries of Germany were breathtaking, so I took note of whatever captured my attention. Germany has lush green grass and towering thick woods---an extreme opposite of the environment of the Philippines. I was in shock. I couldn't believe everything was so green and lush. I wondered why illegal loggers had destroyed the forest in the Philippines. Moreover, I was in awe of the beautiful man-made structures that were nestled across the German countryside; it was as if it was a continuous painting right out of a story book. With all the surroundings, the four-hour journey did not seem that long.

Michelle Fernandez Cendaña

## At first duty station in Augsburg, Bavaria

We arrived at Sheridan Kaserne in Augsburg around five o'clock in the afternoon. As we got out of the van, with my German phrase book in my hand, I wanted to thank the driver in German but I couldn't get myself to say "Danke Schoen" (Thank you in a beautiful way). Instead, even after hours of practice, I said thank you in English and the driver smiled. I felt horrible that I couldn't thank him in his own language. Before I could beat myself up, I quickly walked to our organization's headquarters to report so the company I was assigned to could pick me up.

Sergeant Jones, my would-be boss, picked me up and introduced me to the Company First Sergeant. The first sergeant loaned me his radio and told me that if I needed anything, I just had to let him know. I thought it was strange but I took the radio as I like having a little pleasant background noise in my room. I was introduced to the Supply Sergeant who issued me bedding. Sergeant Jones took me to the shoppette (a small military store comparable to corner stores) so I could have something to eat for dinner. Later, the sergeant took me to my barracks room and mentioned that he would pick me up early the next day to start in-processing at the installation. I couldn't sleep that night not only because of jetlag, but also because the sun didn't set until 11pm.

The morning came and I felt I was ready to meet a new day. Sergeant Jones showed up in the barracks along with another person who was my military sponsor, Specialist Dorothy Hagler. She showed me around and ensured that I was well taken care of. She introduced me to our company commander who gave me an initial appreciation for Bavaria by vividly describing its beautiful scenery. Since I arrived on the 2nd of July, a four-day weekend was well under way for the 4th of July. Specialist Hagler took me with her children to one of Germany's oldest cities, Rothenburg ob der Tauberg. I owe this lady so much, but she never asked for anything in return.

For a week, I never did anything work-related, but focused on getting to know the community and German life and culture. We sat in classrooms receiving briefings one after another and went out to lunch in local German restaurants. We also studied German traffic laws to get ready for the driver licensing exams. I realized that we, members of the American Forces were extremely privileged; we didn't have to go through what the Germans go through in order to get their driver license. I'd heard that for the Germans, it was mandatory for them to take 'Fahrschule' or driving school and pay at least 3,500 Deutsche Mark. We Americans took only a written test and most if not all of us passed the first time.

First Sunday worship service that led to wonderful friends

When I first arrive at a new military duty station, I immediately check out two things: first is the church schedule and second is the library schedule. On my first Sunday in Germany, I knew I wanted to attend a military church service. I scanned through my new soldier welcome packet to find potential locations and start times. I found one; it was a Protestant service starting at 10:30 in the morning. To ensure I was on time for church, I did a route recon or in other words walked the entire 1 mile route the day before to ensure I knew where I was going. That Sunday the wind was brisk, but at that moment that wasn't a problem since I only had a short walk to the chapel. However, once I stepped inside the building, the lights were off and there was no one inside. Confused, I stepped out of the building and looked around and spotted a number of people wearing long dresses, heavy coats and holding Bibles in their hands. I blindly followed them to a gathering of people on a sports field seated on bleachers; the service was going to be outdoors. Determined to hear the word of God, I mentally prepared myself for the cold. A warming moment from the church service occurred at the first hymnal song of the morning. Unfortunately, I didn't bring a Bible or a hymnal with me to church. As the congregation was about to start singing, a lady who looked Filipino stepped closer to me in order to share her hymnal. It was cold outside, but at that moment, I felt welcomed and was glad for the gratitude from this woman.

At the conclusion of the service, the lady, who introduced herself as Jhing, asked me if I were Filipino and the minute I said yes, she started speaking with me in Tagalog. She is an older woman, but very youthful and immediately befriended me. Ate Jhing introduced me to the ladies of the chapel. As I was introduced, I found it hilarious that the ladies thought I was Ate Jhing's daughter. In response, Ate Jhing said that if she had a daughter, then she would have liked to have one like me.

As days went by, I also met Ate Jhing's husband, Doug Wiest. With the couple, I went on Volksmarches to Austria and Switzerland. On a number of occasions, we went on trips to Munich and Augsburg. Ate Jhing and Doug were extremely nice to me and we all had a great time.

Ate Jhing and I usually ate at Pizza Hut or other fast food joints after church. This tradition reminded me of my time after church in the Philippines where I used to walk, talk and eat with my grandmother, great aunts and cousins. Even though I was far away from friends and family, God provided friends and family at that current place and time. For the provisions of friends and family, I must say that wherever God sends me, He meets my needs.

## Work at the motor pool

I worked at the Headquarters and Service Company (HSC), 527th Military Intelligence Battalion motor pool, which was a five-minute walk from my barracks room. At 6:30am, the HSC soldiers had a formation and we participated in physical fitness training for an hour. By 7:30am, physical fitness was over and we usually walked for

10 minutes to the dining hall to eat breakfast. Thereafter, we would get ready for work in the barracks and we were at work by 9:00am. Work entailed sitting behind a computer and inputting supply requests. At the time, the Army was still using legacy computer systems, which were unable to transfer files from one computer to another across the Internet. To update my computer system, I took my only break of the day to walk or to drive to the local logistics support depot to transport computer update disks and to pick up vehicle parts.

Monday was the battalion maintenance day and soldiers would come in to my office and pick up their vehicle keys and maintenance checklist to dispatch their vehicles. Needless to say, I was well known as the Prescribed Load List (PLL) clerk or the "dispatcher" at the motor pool. I was a private (E-2) then and I got used to my dispatcher title after a while especially when my fellow soldiers couldn't properly pronounce my name. "Private C, can I get a dispatch?" That was the usual request. After working for four months at the motor pool, I became good at ordering parts and issuing dispatches. Some soldiers were amazed at how well I could recite stock numbers when they came in to ask for vehicle parts. The simple fact was that after repeatedly ordering the same parts, I was just familiar with the numbers. However, the mechanics were not amazed because they expected me to know all of the stock numbers. Many of the mechanics used to compare me with previous clerks who would memorize every single string of stock numbers. I did not have the inclination nor did I see the necessity to memorize stock numbers.

To break the monotony of the work week, I used to go to the USO (United Services Organization) office to look for weekend express trips. With private E-2 pay, I tried my hardest to go on tours and see other European countries. During my second month in Germany, I booked my first trip to Nove, Italy. Since my birthday was in August and the trip was during the same month, the USO travel representative gave me a 50% discount. Unfortunately, the trip was cancelled due to the lack of participation. I was almost disappointed until the travel representative at the office said that I could use my reservation for the next month's trip without an additional fee. The next month, I ended up going to Paris, one of the world's most romantic destinations.

On the bus, I arrived early in the morning to Paris. With the Notre Dame Cathedral in view, I asked myself, "Who would have known I would visit Paris?" I was in awe of the beauty of the city and I thanked the Lord for allowing me to see Paris. We spent nine hours in Paris, and my newfound friends and I never took a break from walking and sightseeing. I returned to Augsburg with my heart full of joy and contentment.

## Attendance to a certification course in Vilseck

After an inspection that was conducted on our office, my supervisor realized that I needed to be certified to work there. Consequently, for a week, I went to a course along with two Sergeants to Vilseck, a four hour drive towards Eastern Bavaria. One of the two sergeants named Sergeant Luce took me under his wing while we were there. He gave me a ride there and back and gave me his insight about how to do well in the Army

When I arrived to Vilseck, the guesthouse on the military post was already booked. The guesthouse receptionist allowed me to stay off post in a nice German guesthouse instead. To me the experience was like a mini-vacation. Once the class was over and I had dinner with the other sergeants, I had time to read and watch TV in my hotel room.

Each morning during the drive to class, I always had questions about life in the military. SGT Luce never got tired of answering my questions and was always happy to talk about his family and his experience in the military. I think I learned more from the conversations with SGT Luce than I had learned from my class. Sergeant Luce loved his family and enjoyed serving in the Army so much that it was inspiring to me.

I enjoyed the little get away to Vilseck especially with the snow fall and the beauty of the countryside. Nearly every day, SGT Luce and I would visit the military electronics store called the "Powerzone." There I'd lose myself looking at new gadgets and movies. Since there wasn't much to do once we had left post, I would stay in my room and write to family and friends or just relax and get ready for the next day. Often, I would ask myself why the Lord blessed me.

Returning to work with more insight

Once I got back to work, everyone was glad to see me. At first, I thought they were joking around because my job was only to issue out vehicle keys but I noticed true sincerity from the soldiers. Little by little, I was making friends with my fellow soldiers. Soon, I had even attracted the attention of a male soldier. Before I knew it, he had become my first boyfriend. Sadly, the relationship only lasted three months, but along the way, I learned how to connect with people again.

In addition to friends, I had a number of mentors who also shaped my personal development. One of the most memorable was Staff Sergeant Frank J. Berry. He had a no nonsense attitude and positive perspective. Staff Sergeant Berry was able to recognize when I was frustrated at work and was quick to offer words of encouragement. He took a special interest in molding me to become a better person. Staff Sergeant Berry was one of the people that the Lord strategically placed in my path that encouraged me to be a good soldier.

The lessons I learned in the class at Vilseck gave me a confidence boost because it reinforced some of the skills that were required in my job. SGT Jones, my immediate supervisor, began to notice that I was able to process parts requests faster than before I attended the class. Additionally, he commented on my fast typing abilities. I explained that I used to take typing classes in the Philippines where the teachers were so strict that if students were caught looking at the keyboard, the teachers would send the students out of the classroom as punishment. Intrigued by my story, SGT Jones developed a curiosity about the Philippines. I didn't mind sharing anything with anyone who wanted to know more about the country where I was born and raised.

At one point, my boss asked if the houses in the Philippines were huts. I laughed. Immediately, I thought of island movies that perhaps, in people's minds, accurately depict reality in countries such as the Philippines. I explained to my boss that as much as it is true that there are huts, most houses in the Philippines are made of concrete. In reflection, my officemates had different perspectives that fueled my own curiosity about the world. The office had become a fun place to learn about new cultures.


## Making friends that would last a lifetime

In November 1996, a Caucasian gentleman dressed in business casual attire walked into my office and asked for a vehicle dispatch. I assumed that he was a civilian until he handed me his military driver's license. I looked at his license and found that he was a Staff Sergeant. A brief moment later, after I returned his identification, he asked me if I was Filipino. Surprised that he recognized my nationality, I answered him straightforwardly. He told me that he was married to a Filipino named Juliet and that his name was Staff Sergeant Larry Isgrig. He left me his home phone number and he invited me to his house on Thanksgiving Day so I could meet his family.

Thanksgiving dinner came and I remembered walking for about 15 minutes in the snow trying to get to Staff Sergeant Isgrig's apartment in the military housing compound. The moment I walked in to Staff Sergeant

Isgrig's home, I knew he had a wonderful family. He and his wife had two kids, Kevin and Kristina. Each family member played a part in preparing for the Thanksgiving meal. The dinner consisted of traditional Filipino dishes and desserts. I was also able to enjoy the company of several other family friends during the Thanksgiving meal. The Isgrig's took me in like a member of their family, even the children called me "Auntie Michelle." Together, we made countless trips to Post Exchanges (military department store) and PowerZones at various military installations. Plus we spent quality time at theme parks and traveled together to Venice, Italy. The Isgrig family helped me create beautiful memories of Germany and even now that we are thousands of miles apart, we remain in touch.

## Promotion to Private First Class

Normally, soldiers get promoted to PFC in the US Army within their 12 months of service. As of November 1996, I had been in the Army for nearly 13 months and I still was not promoted. Specialist Cimo, a frequent visitor to my dispatch desk, asked about my promotion status. Every week, he would ask me when my supervisor was going to recommend me for promotion from Private E-2 to Private First Class. He suggested that I ask my boss for a promotion and even gave me pointers on how to ask.

I kept asking my immediate supervisor when I should expect to be promoted. My supervisor normally responded with "I will get back with you." Frustrated, I usually went home from work wondering why I wasn't promoted. On several occasions, I wished that I had been in trouble that would have merited punishment so at least there was a reason I wasn't promoted. In my mind, I was a hardworking person who never got in trouble and one who my supervisor should recommend to the commander for promotion.

I turned to the Lord in prayer and left the situation in His hands. Quite interestingly, one afternoon in late

December of that same year, my supervisor walked into the office saying he had headaches and didn't seem to be in a good mood. When I had asked what happened, he said, "I wanted to appear before the Staff Sergeant Promotion Board but they wouldn't let me." For a second, I felt sorry for him then I thought to myself "This guy cares about his promotion, but doesn't care about mine." Later, I asked, "SGT, when will I get promoted to PFC? This will be the 13$^{th}$ month I've been in the military." In reply, he said, "Oh, I'm sorry Cendaña; I thought you came to Germany as Private E-1." So much for paying attention, I thought. This guy saw me every day and never noticed the rank on my collar which was a measly little subdued private rank that looked like a broken wing of a mosquito. Moreover, he typed my personal/professional growth counseling monthly where he had to type my rank and it never dawned on him that my next logical rank was PFC. I was infuriated, but didn't show it. Out of curiosity, I asked one of the Staff Sergeants I came to know and trust why my supervisor wasn't allowed to go to the board. He said, "Cendaña, we notice everything. He is not being sent because he is lazy." Sufficient answer and well put, I thought. After a long and invisible battle, I became a PFC.


## Taking classes with the University of Maryland, Europe

After six months of doing my job, I felt comfortable pursuing other activities outside of work. I walked into the Education Center to check what classes were offered for the next term. I had no doubt that I would enroll. Once there, I was a bit intimidated by the school's name, but then I thought, "Hmmm, I finished my first year of college in the Philippines successfully so why shouldn't I try." The school, at the time, was offering my favorite class, Public Speaking.

Convinced that I would enroll, I grabbed application forms. After filling them out, I spoke with the Field Representative of the school and she asked for my high school transcripts and asked if I had taken the Test of English as a Foreign Language (TOEFL). I was stumped. I told her that I graduated in the Philippines and didn't have my transcript with me. However, I told her that Hawaii Pacific University evaluated my transcript when I joined the Army and according to that school, my high school credits were equivalent to that of US high schools. With regard to taking TOEFL, I told her that I would take it as soon as possible in Heidelberg, a four-hour drive away from Augsburg.

The representative phoned the school's headquarters in Heidelberg. Although I couldn't hear the voice on the other line, I could deduce what they were discussing about based on the responses I was hearing from the field representative. At one point, the representative said, "I don't see that being a problem. She [referring to me] was just speaking with me." I thought, "Ah, the other person on the line is wondering if I could speak English well enough to be enrolled in the course." With the approval of the school's headquarters, I took courses under academic probation.

I was extremely excited to be able to enroll into my class. Fortunately, the Army's Tuition Assistance Program paid for 75% of the course. Therefore, I only had to pay the small cost difference and for the class textbook. I ended up tremendously enjoying the class. While I disliked writing and doing research for my speeches, I found the delivery portion of a speech to be exhilarating. Similar to high school, I was performing on stage but on a smaller scale. I wrote and delivered different types of speeches that had to be either informative, persuasive or commemorative. Although, I had fun in most of my class sessions, I found out that after my persuasive speech on a fairly controversial topic, one of my classmates took the speech personally, and started spreading rumors that I was vain and distasteful. I was shocked and I couldn't believe that someone would make up rumors and think that I was a bad person simply because they disagreed with my perspective. I laughed at her reaction as I never intended to target or offend anyone.

Over the course of my assignment in Germany, I earnestly took classes. I realized that in all my life, I had been competing to be the best academically and I would cut corners to reach the top. But this time, I wanted to do everything right; no cheating and no competing with others. If I had to compete, I was only going to compete with myself. Before taking classes at the University of Maryland, I enjoyed relaxing after work and sleeping in on the weekends. However, with class there was a lot of sacrifice of my time, my social life and many hours of sleep. With God's grace and mercy, my efforts were not in vain.

I received a congratulatory letter in the mail from the University of Maryland stating that I made the dean's list. In disbelief, I called the school's headquarters in Heidelberg to verify that the administration had not made a mistake. I asked one of the administrators, "How could this be? I am on academic probation. I haven't taken the TOEFL." The lady checked my records and sure enough I was right, but she said, "I'm placing you in our records as a regular student. You're no longer required to take TOEFL and congratulations on making the dean's list." That was the highlight of my week.


## Appearance at Soldier Boards

The Lord had slowly been easing my anxiety and self-doubt. Before joining the Army, the menial jobs I had in Hawaii had a negative effect on me and my family because the jobs were not challenging and my family felt that the work was putting a damper on my future. However, each success I made in the Army started to build my self-confidence. To gauge the growth of my self-confidence in the Army, I decided to compete at a Soldier of the Month Board. These boards are interviews that test a soldier's military knowledge and also serves as a uniform inspection session. Senior military soldiers panel the boards and determine the top competitor. I felt that if I do well I could potentially set myself up for future promotion, but have a solid indication that I can do well at something if I persevere.

My first board was at the company level (a military organization that consists of about 130 soldiers). I won this board and I continued to study for the Soldier of the Quarter for the battalion, the next military echelon. At the battalion board, I won by default because no one else showed up but still had to face the formal board of interviewers. Not long after the Quarter Board, I competitively won the Battalion Soldier of the Year Board against three other soldiers. The boards gave me a confidence boost and put me ahead of my peers. Unbeknownst to me, my Platoon Sergeant, Sergeant First Class Winkles put me in for an early promotion waiver for the rank of Specialist without the knowledge of my direct supervisor. Surprisingly, after four months as a Private First Class, I received my promotion to Specialist.

The Lord gave me the strength to carry on with work, school and the boards, but I knew in my heart that studying for soldier boards took the highest priority in all my activities. My boyfriend at the time helped me study everyday and put things in perspective. He saw that I was stressed and would take me out for a walk in late afternoons or for a run early in the morning before accountability formation. There was a time during my preparation for the brigade soldier board that I entertained the thought of losing so I could devote some of my time to my classes. Nevertheless, I decided to continue to study and attempt to win the Brigade Soldier of the Year. I lost in that competition but it led to opportunities that I did not expect.

Unexpectectly, after becoming the runner up for the brigade soldier board, the members of the board chose my speech on Army Values to be the best among all who participated. The board members told me that I had to redeliver my speech in public during the awards ceremony with our Brigade Commander as one of the audience. The speech was well put together given the fact that there were three Noncommissioned Officers who helped me produce it. Our Brigade Commander appreciated the speech and asked if

Michelle Fernandez Cendaña

I would like to deliver it in front of generals. Needless to say, I was intimidated so I told her that she was entitled to the speech and to do with it whatever she pleased.

Typically, me and my fellow soldiers, who work in the motor pool, were thought of as less smarter than Military Intelligence (MI) soldiers. This perspective stemmed from that fact that the standardized military occupational test requirement for MI is higher than that of mechanics. Though many soldiers were in denial, the truth of the matter was some of the mechanics scored higher than some MI soldiers. After my delivery of my speech on Army Values, soldiers of various ranks looked at me and my fellow workers in the motor pool in a different light. My speech garnered a little bit more respect from soldiers who were in the MI field.

The speech also made a tremendous impact on my image in the unit as well. The Brigade Commander was searching for a new driver and she specifically asked for me by name to interview. I had wondered if it was because I could write or deliver a speech because it seemed odd that any of these talents had anything to do with being her military chauffer. Under the order of the Brigade Command Sergeant Major, I reported to his office for the interview. I wanted the position, but I explained to him that I did not want to put the Brigade Commander's life in danger and regretfully declined the offer. I had one traffic accident on my record and I feared that it might happen again. The Command Sergeant Major reconfirmed my decision and I sharply stood up and left his office. To my utmost relief, another soldier got the job although I felt honored that the Brigade Commander considered me.


Promotion to Sergeant

My preparation for the soldier boards prepared me for the Sergeant Promotion Board. Among everything I had to do to prepare for the promotion board, my supervisor's letter of recommendation was the hardest to obtain. My current supervisor at the time did not want to recommend me because he felt that I was getting promoted too quickly. To delay a direct answer, he would always tell me that he needed to check the guidance from the Army Enlisted Promotion regulation. Little did he know, I already checked the regulation and according to the regulation, I could attend the board if I was granted a waiver.

Soon after competing in the Brigade Soldier of the Year Board, I asked my supervisor when I could attend the promotion board. Throughout the summer of 1997 my supervisors' response to my promotion was always, "I have to check the regulation." When November came, I woke up and told myself that I couldn't take the same reply anymore. I cornered my boss and asked for the exact reasons why I shouldn't appear before the board. Sensing my seriousness, he left the office and said that he would immediately address the situation with his boss.

Within a few minutes, my supervisor returned, and he told me that his boss, SFC Coleman, told him that I was not ready for the promotion board. Furthermore, SFC Coleman instructed my supervisor to generate a counseling form with this assessment in case I wanted an opportunity to formally rebut the promotion assessment. Half-jokingly, my supervisor told me that if I got promoted too quickly I might find myself in a leadership position without knowing anything about the military. Needless to say, I was angry, but I allowed the comments to soak in my memory for a couple of moments. The same day, at lunchtime, I heard SFC Coleman's voice in the office next door and I decided to seize the moment and confront SFC Coleman directly about my promotion.

Barging into the office, I angrily asked questions I normally wouldn't ask. I said, "Sergeant, am I getting punished for striving for excellence? I wonder why I am not getting sent to the promotion board." Keeping his cool, SFC Coleman laughed and said, "No, no, Cendaña, your supervisor walked into my office saying that you are not ready to go to the board." Furthermore, SFC Coleman said,

"Okay; with or without your supervisor's approval, you are going to the promotion board next month." It was such a relief, but I couldn't believe that I always had to fight for what I wanted.

By December, my supervisor had not completed my promotion paperwork packet. Consequently, I could not go to the promotion board for that month. Looking at the situation from a positive perspective, I was profoundly grateful for the extra time that I could spend on studying for the following board in January. My aim and prayer at the time, if it was the Lord's will, was to score the maximum points possible at the promotion board. When January rolled around and the board finally convened, I walked out of the room feeling content with my performance. When the board released the final performance scores, I couldn't believe my eyes – I scored 199 out of a possible 200. One of the First Sergeants on the promotion board told me that I was only the second person during his entire tenure in the battalion to receive such a high score from a promotion board.

The next step in the promotion process was frustrating. Promotion board results take three months for the process through the promotion system. Each month, the Army posts cut off scores for promotion. The month following my board, I glanced through a copy of the Army Times newspaper to assess the trend in promotion cut off scores. The cut-off score for my MOS was in the low 600s out of a possible 800. My overall promotion score at the time was 590. I silently prayed telling God that my promotion was in His hands.

I knew that the Lord does not withhold what is best for us as stated in James 1:17, "Every good and perfect gift is from above, coming down from the Father of the heavenly lights, who does not change like shifting shadows." I only had to believe. On the month that my promotion scores were effective, the cut-off score was exactly at 590. One of our brigade administrative specialists broke the news to me as soon as the Army published the official list. I was in awe of God's miracle. Vividly, I said, "Lord, you picked me up from where I was." I could have missed God's blessing if I started to take extra classes and correspondence courses to boost my promotion score. I was profoundly grateful to the Lord at that very moment.

I earned my Sergeant's stripes on June 5, 1998 after graduating from the 30-day leadership training at Grafenwoehr, Germany. Once I made the promotion points list, I had one year to attend the mandatory leadership training or else I would forfeit my promotion. The training in Grafenwoehr was both exciting and challenging. I gained additional insight from the training on what type of leader I wanted to become; one that was firm, but fair.

Due to hard work, I earned the promotion to Sergeant with exactly two and a half years of military service. A number of soldiers speculated that I had slept around to gain promotions. I made it clear that God looked favorably upon working hard and doing the right things. He empowered me to be a fulltime soldier who studied and set priorities towards promotion. To those who believe in God, their promotion is in God's hands; His perfect orchestration will manifest in unexpected ways.

## Foreign Service Tour Extension

I came down on orders to Fort Hood, Texas; my two-year assignment to Germany had come to a close. I had almost embraced the fact that I was moving to Texas, until my Company Commander told me that with my organization's move from Augsburg to Darmstadt, the unit needed my job specialty. If I elected to stay in Germany, my assignment to Texas would be rescinded. I had one night to decide upon my fate for the next two years. I prayed over the decision-making process and wrote down advantages and disadvantages for both options. Surprisingly, I couldn't find any reason to leave Germany. Therefore, the next morning, I went to my unit Career Counselor and extended myself for another two-year assignment in Germany. Off to Darmstadt I moved.

# Chapter 6

## Return to "Paradise": Total Rejection

*"See, I have engraved you on the palms of my hands." Isaiah 49:16*

Since my move from Augsburg, spiritual and other aspects of my life began to change in ways I never imagined. I began to attend a church called World Harvest Christian International Center; a place where I saw God's love in action. I experienced God's anointing through sermons, praise, and worship. I wondered in anticipation what God would do next in my life.

My time in Germany quickly passed by without me realizing it due to great experiences I had with my church, family and friends. With my close friends Matthew Balz, whom I call "Bro", and Song Gunter, my roommate, I had a group of people that I enjoyed spending time with after work. Most of the time, I hung out with Bro. As we were both Sergeants, we used to eat together, take classes together and discuss the things we were capable of doing. He used to say, "Michelle, given the proper education and training, we both can do what the lieutenants and officers are doing." Bro's comments made me want to push myself as a soldier to become an officer. On the weekends, the Isgrigs and Wiests families took me in like a daughter and we all had a great time traveling and regularly visiting Post Exchanges. Although I had enjoyed my time with my new found family, I began to think about going back to Hawaii after my sister told me she was expecting a child. It had been nearly three and a half years since I was in Hawaii and not only did I want to see my sister through childbirth but also want to see my little cousin Sharmaine's christening. With both upcoming events occurring, I thought that it must be the perfect time to go back.

## Return to Hawaii

It was March 1999 when I requested to take leave for 30 days to be by my sister's side when she gave birth to her daughter, Yasmeen, and to attend my goddaughter, Sharmaine's Christening and birthday party. On the plane from Frankfurt International Airport, I was thinking about what it would be like again to be back home. Had anything changed since I'd been gone? With an 18-hour flight, I had plenty of time to think through my situation in Hawaii. I left at 19 and was finally returning at 22. When I had left I did not have the best relationship with my mom. Combined with making a good impression with everyone and working two jobs, I felt I had room to grow in building a stronger bond with my family in Hawaii. I prayed to the Lord for wisdom and maturity to look at everything in a renewed light.

After a long flight, I finally arrived at Honolulu International Airport smelling the pleasant Hawaiian breeze. My pregnant sister and her husband, Kuya Dante, picked me up from the airport. The ride home was short, because they only lived two blocks away from the airport. Since we hadn't seen each other in awhile, my sister and I ended up talking until 3 in the morning. Due to our long conversation and hours of jet-lag, I didn't wake up until 4:00pm the next day. While I was sleeping, my brother in-law jokingly asked my sister, "Is she still alive?" She laughed and left to check on me to find that I was still sound asleep. When I finally awoke, my sister asked me what I wanted to eat. I had a craving for a good American pizza from Pizza Hut. When I told my sister that I wanted to eat pizza, she looked at me strangely and asked if Kuya Dante encouraged me to tell her that I wanted pizza for dinner. When I told her that my craving was my own, she then explained that she had restricted Kuya Dante from eating pizza because of his health.

I stayed a few days on Oahu before I flew to Maui. My stay there was long enough for my brother in-law to come up with a nickname for me, which was 'String Bean' or just 'String.' With my camera equipment ready, I was excited to get back to Maui. Wearing a sleeveless top and a pair of shorts with my hair down, my mom almost didn't recognize me. I was so pale that she said I looked like I was Japanese. I laughed. After we left the airport, my mom drove me straight to her favorite Chinese restaurant in Wailuku where we enjoyed a good conversation and caught up on lost times.

Two days after my arrival to Maui, I went to my cousin Sharmaine's birthday celebration at the Lahaina Civic Center. On the night of the event, I hesitatingly entered the hall. I was away from the islands for so long that it took several moments for my relatives to recognize me. A few minutes later, I was surrounded by my extended family and they all gave me hugs and kisses, and bombarded me with questions. I felt a little uneasy at the time because I hate being the center of attention. Aunt Christy, one of my biological mother's best friends, started to cry and said that I reminded her of my mother. I remembered a picture I had of her and thought I looked more like my grandmother. However, I completely understood what Aunt Christy was thinking.

The first few days of my vacation were great; there were many days of fun and excitement. Unfortunately, as time passed, Mom and I were not getting along as great as I had planned. Being out of the house for some time, I had gotten used to a certain level of independence. In order to prevent any other disagreements with my mom, I cut my vacation by a couple of days in order to give everyone space. I was a little sad that by leaving early, I missed my niece's birth, but I was happy to be able to spend some time with both my close and extended family.

## A new beginning

At Frankfurt International Airport, I called Staff Sergeant Isgrig to see if he could pick me up. Thirty minutes later, he was there, and he brought me back to Darmstadt. Both him and my platoon sergeant were surprised to see me so soon. I told them both that my mom and I had a disagreement so I thought it was best for me to come back to Germany. Staff Sergeant Isgrig and my platoon sergeant both gave me advice to move on and focus on what I could control. I then focused my attention and energy on work, school and Non-Commissioned Officer Boards.

Moreover, Matthew also helped me put things into perspective so that I looked at the positive things that were happening to me in my career in the Army. I thanked God that I had a friend like him who was a constant source of encouragement and endless laughter.


## 1999 INSCOM NCO of the Year, Atlantic Region

Over the next couple of months, I participated in several competitive soldier boards. With God's grace, in the summer of 1999, I won the Intelligence and Security Command's (INSCOM) Non-Commissioned Officer of the Year for the European region. Surprisingly, I was the only non-Military Intelligence soldier that competed. I praised the Lord to have had the opportunity to compete at that level.

Later that year, I flew to Fort Belvoir, Virginia to compete for the overall INSCOM NCO of the Year. During the flight to the US, I intensely studied and prepared for the competition, which unfortunately led to intense headaches and sleep problems during my trip. In retrospect, I probably should have relaxed because there was plenty of time in the competition schedule to do last minute studying.

Aside from the competition, the organizer of the event took us to the home of the INSCOM Commanding General, Major General Noonan. The general briefly spoke with us and surprisingly took time to recognize me for having competed with all MI soldiers and made it to the INSCOM level. On another day of my trip, the organizers took us to Gettysburg, Pennsylvania and gave us a professional development brief on the Battle of Gettysburg.

At that time, I still thought in my Philippine dialect and found myself mentally translating to English to get my point across. During my final board competition, I was asked several questions in which I wished I could have answered in my own dialect. There were several answer choices that I could have mentioned but for some reason I could not translate my responses into English quick enough. Consequently, to the board members, I looked ill-prepared. I lost the competition but I gave it my best and that's what mattered to me. I also learned a valuable lesson on how to persevere.


## A test of my faith in God

In the midst of my closer relationship with the Lord, my faith was tested. In early December 1999, the unexpected arose — my skin allergy came back. Far more irritating and severe than the typical chicken pox infection, my skin allergy kept me incapacitated for nearly three days. Moreover, I completed a medical lab test for my Green to Gold officer application, which revealed that I had borderline blood cholesterol and high blood pressure. I couldn't believe the results and felt even worse about the news since I was still recovering from my skin allergy outbreak. Sadly, a few days after receiving my sobering blood cholesterol results, my brother in-law e-mailed me that my mom had a heart attack.

I had to go home to see my mom. I dreaded the 18-hour flight and nearly cried on the plane because I had to keep going to the aircraft lavatory to apply various medications on my entire body. Overall, the experience was torture.

When I arrived in Honolulu, I was not much of a help to my family since I kept going back to the Army hospital to recover from my own skin problems. To help with the pain, the doctors put me on prescription steroids. Almost overnight, my skin infections subsided and I became calm and relaxed. Thank God, I was much more passive and did not overreact when I saw that my Mom was in the hospital for a heart attack.

The next two weeks was a trying situation for everyone in the family. Fortunately, Mom was released from the hospital before Christmas and the family celebrated Christmas and New Year's quietly at my sister's house. I went back to Germany feeling a little better and I made a conscious decision to take good care of myself and leave every burden I was carrying in God's hands. The Lord, the great physician, healed me from my afflictions.

# Chapter 7

## Pursuing my Academic Dream

*"The Lord Himself goes before you and will be with you; he will never leave you nor forsake you. Do not be afraid; do not be discouraged." Deuteronomy 31:8*

<u>Getting out of my safety net</u>

I thought I would always stay in the military. In pursuit of realizing my dream to finish college, I finally declared my intent of leaving military active duty status—*my safety net*. In all honesty, my decision to leave the military was rather difficult. I liked being in the Army for it had many benefits. Some of the basic benefits included college tuition assistance, a decent salary, accelerated promotion opportunities, and the ability to take off time to travel. Above all benefits provided by the Army, I was always afforded the time to worship and give praise to the Lord. No matter how intense the training was, my military leadership ensured that I could attend church services. While some people may have developed bitterness towards the Army, I had unexpectedly found myself happy to be a part of it.

Never in my wildest dreams did I plan or even imagine myself wearing the camouflage pattern uniform. It just happened. All I recall was my impassioned prayer to God to be able to go back to college full time in 1994. Ironically, over a year later, I found myself in the Army trying to fit in the ranks of the bold and the brave. I feared the unknown. I prayed and wept over my decision. In the midst of a challenging basic combat training, I thought I would not be able to make it. Although I did not understand it at first, I realized that the plight drew me nearer to God. At that point in my life, our Father in Heaven showed me His awesome faithfulness. He absolutely does not leave nor forsake His children. Another lesson that I learned was the attitude I had been praying for—that He would humble me in all my ways. Going through all the hardships humbled me.

For most of 1999 I had worked on my Green to Gold packet. I was counting on the Green to Gold program to get into college. I was able to get profound and cogent letters of recommendation from my company and battalion commanders and the Professor of Military Science at the University of Iowa. By March of 2000 I was still working on becoming a US citizen, I only needed my certificate of naturalization from the citizenship process to complete my Green to Gold packet. To help expedite the process, I sought the assistance from a Hawaii Senator. However, his staff's assistance was unable to make a difference. I became frustrated because the processing of my paperwork was beyond my control. And sadly, by the deadline, I did not have the certificate and I was stuck with the options of either re-enlisting into the military or leaving military service. Undecided, I called one of my aunts in the states to discuss my situation and cried like a river.

Leaving active duty was not easy for me especially when my Chain of Command began to offer me incentives to stay in the military. Out of all the promises I was made, two things that would have kept me in, was an assignment to Washington D.C. and the opportunity to teach at my military occupational school. Unfortunately, my career manager could not get me the two incentives that I desired. My chain of command wanted to retain me in the unit and they were not satisfied with the result of the efforts of my career manager. Consequently, my Chain of Command brought it up to the commanding general to intervene. Considering that this commanding general knew me from my performance at the INSCOM NCO of the Year competition, my Chain of Command hoped that he could help me out.

Michelle Fernandez Cendaña

After a few months of waiting, I decided to leave active duty and just serve in the Army National Guard because as a contract option I could still attend a occupational instructor training course in Germany. While in school in Germany, I received a phone call from my career manager informing me that he had an alternate assignment for me that was close to Washington DC. I cordially told him that I was going to remain in the National Guard because I had already arranged to attend school full time. The Iowa Army National Guard gave me flexibility to take a full load of academic courses because the National Guard only required my service one weekend a month and two weeks a year.

After four years of having been pampered in the Army, it seemed like I forgot how to be a civilian again. In the military, I had gotten used to a regimented lifestyle. Standing on my own appeared to be arduous. I knew no one in Iowa. Yet, what scared me the most was the out-of-state tuition. There were times when I told myself that I should have planned to attend the University of Hawaii at Manoa. My tuition would have been at least $7,000 less than the University of Iowa since I was a resident of Hawaii. Believe it or not though, something drew me to the Midwest.

My aunt was nice enough to tell me that I should not consider it a failure when the Green to Gold Program did not work out for me. I reacted that way at first. Certainly, I had the option to accept the assignment and patiently wait for the next school year to qualify for Green to Gold. After giving my options thought and prayer, I chose to attend the University of Iowa that fall semester.


## Ask in the name of Jesus and consider it done

In Mark 11:24 it says, *"Therefore I tell you, whatever you ask for in prayer, believe that you have received it, and it will be yours."* God will always show His grace and mercy through our prayers as long as *"we do not regard iniquity in our hearts"* [see Psalm 66:18]. He is the God who makes a way where there seems to be no way. This will be my testimony to you. The Lord opened doors for me to go back to college. I mentioned before that I petitioned God that I may attain my educational goals yet I ended up in the military. As I analyzed what had happened, the military was a major part of the process. Had I not joined the military, I could never have attended the University of Maryland, European Division, which enabled me to transfer to the University of Iowa.

As soon as I got my financial aid packet from the University of Iowa, I expected that it carried great news. My heart was overjoyed and my mouth could only utter words of praises and thanks to the Lord. God met in various ways my estimated cost of attendance of $20,516 for that school year. He is Jehovah Jireh who deserves all glory, power, honor and praise.

## God straightened my plan

As I thought of my upcoming expenses in Iowa, I considered modeling, a suggestion my friend Anna made to me over two years ago. When Anna originally suggested that I model I laughed in disbelief. I stopped my grinning when I sensed her seriousness, and now thought that modeling might help defray my college expenses.

Additionally, when I was still on the mindset of pursuing Green to Gold, one of my aunts in Hawaii suggested out of the blue that I pose for Calendar Girl. I reacted to her comment the same way I did with Anna. Yet, like Anna, my aunt was dead serious. Without further consideration, I then decided that I would model once I started college as a source of income. However, I did not ask God in prayer if it was His will for me to do it. Soon after considering to model in college, He showed me that I made a bad decision.

Six months right before I was about to start school, my skin allergies became severe. I got down on my knees and asked God to forgive me and I promised I would never use the beauty that He bestowed upon me to bring dishonor to Jesus.

I shared this experience with brother James in church, after stating that God straightened my plan. James said, "Yeah, you have that mole above your lips as your asset." In addition, I told my Uncle Wilson in the Philippines about this over the phone and he laughed at me and implied that I was too short to be model. He told me that I might qualify to model a fish sauce product. I just laughed at his comment.

## The Lord fulfilled His promise

As soon as I got out of the military, I went on vacation to my cousin Sarah's house who lived in Naperville, Illinois. Kuya Mason and Mason B picked me up at Chicago O'Hare International Airport. It had been five years since I first met the Hallett family and it was a great reunion. Also, this was the first time I met my cousin Christine who was four years old.

They had family gatherings which always included me and Krystle, my cousin who was on summer vacation from Maui. My cousins and I visited museums and malls. Since it was summer vacation, Mason B. regularly had baseball games, which we never missed. I remember being the loudest on the bleachers most of the time to cheer on Mason's team and usually people on the bleachers found my enthusiasm to be strange.

I had a wonderful vacation and soon thereafter, I found myself in school. The Lord had fulfilled His promise for me to reach one of my educational goals.

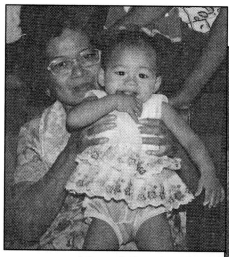

Me and Grandmother

Minerva, my biological
mother

Cinderella
Kindergarten School
Graduation 1982

Salaan Elementary
School Graduation
1989

Mangaldan National
High School
Graduation 1993

On to Iraq
Ramstein, Germany 2005

In a helicopter
Baghdad, Iraq 2006

On Duty
Baghdad, Iraq 2006

Talent Show
Baghdad, Iraq 2006

# Chapter 8

## Philippine Homecoming: Family's Questions

*"He who has the Son has life; he who does not have the Son of God does not have life." 1 John 5:12*

Six months before my graduation from the University of Iowa, I decided to visit my extended family in the Philippines. To get there, it took over 35 hours air travel, but the excitement of seeing relatives whom I hadn't seen in eight years made the travel bearable. Once I arrived at the Ninoy Aquino International Airport in Manila, I knew I was home. My uncles, Jessie and Noel, picked me up from the airport. As we drove through the highways of the Philippines' capital, I looked for the things that were familiar to me. Unfortunately, however, the Shoe Mart North Edsa was the only establishment I could remember.

When I got to Pangasinan (a province that was about three and a half hours drive north of Manila), I knew it was time for me to give full attention to my grandmother who lovingly raised me and to all who awaited my arrival. The great joy I felt seeing my relatives and friends was unfathomable. At last, my dream of being home again came true.

Most of my family in the Philippines get together annually during the Christmas holidays. That year we went to the beach for the family reunion. I had no inclination to swim so I stayed at the cottage guarding and eating the food the family brought to the beach. While I was at the cottage, my Aunt Racquel, who was my biological mother's best friend, approached me about the life I lived in Hawaii.

She asked, "How true were the things we've heard about your difficult experiences in Hawaii?" Understanding that my aunt was getting emotional, I said, "I'm not going to say that what you heard was untrue, but let's just look at what the Lord has done in my life. I have become more matured and He blessed me with much." My aunt cried and asked if I wanted to find out anything about my biological father.

Actually, I have no desire to meet my biological father. I lived in the Philippines for 17 years and no one claimed to be my father. Out of the blue, while I was in Germany, I received a letter from a woman claiming to know my father. In the letter, the woman stated in Tagalog, "I guess it's time for you to know who your father is and that you have five brothers and sisters. Your father is ill and his wife has died. I understand how it is to lose a mother. They need your help."

I told my aunt my thoughts about her question. Without hesitation I said, "My mother died giving birth to me. From what I understand, she died without telling anyone who my father was. Now, if my father knew about me, I don't understand why he never claimed me or took responsibility for his action." In tears, my aunt replied, "Maybe he was young then and didn't know what to do. Also, maybe he was afraid because your grandfather is in politics and your mother's siblings are all men." To her comment I replied, "I believe that if he really cared about me, he wouldn't have feared for his life. Besides, I wouldn't believe that our family would have harmed him if he came forward. I can't find any reason in my heart to meet with him; I have no longing. If what he desires from me is my forgiveness, I have forgiven him a long time ago." My aunt, I believe, was satisfied with my answer and didn't ask any more questions.

While at home, my relatives visited me quite frequently. In between their visits I would work out to stay in shape. Almost every morning, Ate Ester and I went for a run around the neighborhood. We would wake up early around

5:00 to jog and talk. The schedule was perfect for both of us as I was trying to maintain my fitness and she was trying to get fit. Jogging also gave me the opportunity to speak with people whom I met on the streets and who I otherwise would not have had the chance to speak with.

It was not a common occurrence in our community to meet people who love to jog or run. We were drawing attention from just about everybody. It was funny, but after a while I was used to people honking, whistling and smiling at us like we were crazy. I desired to run in a gym on a treadmill so at least I wouldn't be stared at anymore, but to no avail because our community only had two small gym facilities and most of their equipment consisted of weightlifting. So, I continued running outside.

Ate Ester and I spent quality time together talking about God most of the time. She'd heard some of my stories and I told her that had it not been for Christ, I would have been mentally ruined. Truly, I couldn't think of any other way I would have gone through what I went through without Christ. Surprised, Ate Ester didn't expect that I would have faith in God at that level. While growing up in the Philippines, my family didn't really foresee that I would turn up to be devoted to Jesus. Given the mean kid that I was, no one would have expected that I would grow up to be normal or to be a God-revering woman. It's all the Lord's doing and I praise Him for it.

During my vacation, I went back several times to my alma mater, Mangaldan National High School, to visit former teachers and to see what the school looked like since I graduated 14 years ago. The first time I went to visit, the school was closed for the Christmas holidays, but I was happy to be able to see a few of my former teachers. They were the teachers who made great impressions on me. On my second visit, classes were in session. I stayed with Mrs. Clarita Idia in her classroom and she invited me to speak in her English class about my experiences outside of the Philippines. I was in awe of how her students were smart and impressionable. The experience I had in the classroom answering questions or sharing with them my thoughts was something invaluable and memorable to me. The experience made me wish I could return to the Philippines and speak with students more often in the classrooms.

As with the rest of my trip, a number of my cousins and I went to Baguio City just to sightsee. By that time, it had been 15 years since I first visited there and I noticed many differences. There weren't very many pine trees anymore and the aroma that came from the trees no longer overwhelmed the breeze. Nonetheless, many market places of Baguio City still sold the city's trademark goods of strawberry jam and peanut brittle.

Three weeks have come and gone quickly and I thought my adventures from the trip were over. I was wrong. Trouble met me head-on as I was entering the airport's departure terminal. A security guard would not let me pass through security because he believed that I missed my flight as he looked at my ticket.

I rummaged through my carry-on luggage to find my itinerary. Indeed, he was right and I had missed my flight by one day. People usually miss their flight by a few hours and there I was —an exception. I worried that I would not leave that day. All I could think about were my classes that started the following week.

As I attempted to go to the Singapore Airlines office, which was on another wing of the airport, to get my flight changed, a woman security guard sitting on a booth right beside the elevator would not let me through. She was not satisfied just seeing my passport she wanted to hold on to it. I told her that I wouldn't leave my passport with her and that I would come back and give her my driver's license instead.

Fortunately, when I went to get my license from the luggage, my Aunt Noemi told me that the security guard who did not let me enter the first time changed his mind. I believe my aunt sweet-talked him.

Visiting my family put a closure to many of my ex-tended family concerns and gave them peace in knowing I was happy with my life.

# Chapter 9

## Graduating and Commissioning as a Second Lieutenant

*"And we know that in all things God works for the good of those who love him, who have been called according to his purpose." Romans 8:5*

<u>Graduation</u>

I graduated in only two years from the University of Iowa with a Bachelor of Arts due to the large amount of credits transferred from the University of Maryland - University College. I could have stayed at the University of Iowa to take extra classes and to compete to be a honor graduate however, I didn't want to continue paying tuition. I was still considered an out-of-state student and I couldn't rationalize spending another $11,000 on tuition just to take a couple of extra classes. I realized that my primary objective was to earn my bachelors and move on to the next chapter of my life.

The night before graduation I found myself on a small road trip with my cousin Diana. Unfortunately, on the way back home, we became lost. We ended up in an open field at around midnight with no clue where we were.

The rest of my relatives were on their way to a hotel and they did not even know the predicament Ate Diane and I were in. I was just so glad that someone invented cellular phones and that the 911-phone system existed. "What's your emergency?" asked the agent. A little embarrassed I answered, "Not really an emergency, but a semi-emergency. I am stuck in the middle of nowhere and I don't have a map. I am trying to get back to Iowa City." I expected the agent to become angry with me because my case was not really an emergency, but she was actually very helpful. When my cousin and I got to my apartment, I was relieved with the thought that I would make it to my graduation ceremony.

There were four groups of people family and friends that planned to attend my graduation. My family and friends car pooled in several vehicles to the Hawkeye Carver Arena, the place where my graduation ceremony was going to be held. Despite planning, we could not initially find each other and again I was thankful that we all had cell phones which enabled us to meet. With all the chaos and moving around, I lost my cap tassel. Someone was about to go back to my apartment to look for it, but thank God the school had a booth with gowns for sale. The ceremony was long and tedious but I made it through by befriending with my two seatmates who both made ludicrous comments about college life.

Professional photographers took pictures of the graduates individually, which was minutes before we walked across the stage. My turn came to walk the stage and I nearly cried out of joy. Finally, my dream came true. At the moment my diploma was in my hand, I remembered God's word in Isaiah 54:17, "no weapon forged against you will prevail, and you will refute every tongue that accuses you. This is the heritage of the servants of the Lord, and this is their vindication from me." Once I got off the stage, I remembered how God not only brought me to Hawaii, but also to many countries in Europe beyond my wildest dreams. This showed me that men and women may try to discourage you, but no one can stop God in fulfilling His purpose for His children.

After the ceremony, we took plenty of pictures to remember the event. We then headed to my favorite Italian restaurant, *Olive Garden*. There I was bombarded with questions about my life's next steps. I spoke with some certainty about a few of my plans, but was still unclear on when I wanted to get married. Of course, I wanted to have my own family and I pray about it continually, but the only challenge was that I did not know God's timing. I decided I would just go with the flow since I heard it said you cannot really plan when you will have a family; it just comes along.

## More Celebration in Illinois

The day after graduation, I went back to Naperville, Illinois with the rest of my relatives since I had two weeks to wait before I left for my officer training program in Washington State. My cousin Sarah threw a party for me. During the preparation, Christine, Ate Sarah's five-year old daughter at the time, went with us to the store. She saw a graduation bear and then she grabbed my attention. Pointing to the bear she said, "Auntie Michelle, I'd like to buy that for you." I smiled with pleasure as her keen observation amazed me. I told her that it was nice, but she did not need to buy it for me. She insisted and her mom bought it. As we grabbed what we needed from the store, Christine saw a graduation cake and asked her mom to buy it, too. I was getting embarrassed and thought, "Please let's get out of here before Christine sees other things that have to do with graduation." Finally, we left. During the party, my cousin's friends and family showered me with plenty of gifts.

## Training at Ft. Lewis, Washington

On June 5, 2002, I started my officer training program with a five-week National Advanced Leadership Course (NALC). It was training I had been preparing for since my junior year in the Reserve Officer Training Corps(ROTC) program in college. NALC is a prerequisite to becoming a commissioned officer in the U.S. Army for those who are in the ROTC program. At NALC, cadets' leadership abilities and skills are measured through rigorous physical training consisting of confidence courses, leadership reaction courses, written and practical exams in land navigation, swimming, weapons qualification, and squad and platoon situational training exercises.

I thought I was ready for the NALC, but I proved myself wrong after our physical fitness test (comprising push-ups, sit-ups and a 2-mile run). I felt I was in worst physical state and I asked to be taken to the hospital; I had been hospitalized once for dehydration. All I knew was I got extremely dehydrated. Part of me was a little bit worried about going to the hospital because I thought I might be sent home without finishing the training. Fortunately, a captain gave me a choice of going to the hospital or staying in the barracks for "bed rest" so I could continue training the next day. I chose to stay in the barracks. Though I was feeling rested, I felt terrible. I knew that our peer evaluation had just begun and I was already showing a weakness. My battle buddy (an assigned partner everywhere I went except for tests requiring individual effort) from Capital University in Ohio was not pleased to see me drinking Gatorade (any sports drinks and junk foods were forbidden during the first two weeks of our training). When I told her of the situation, however, she became sympathetic.

The memorable experiences I had during this training were the practical test in land navigation and situational training exercises. The land navigation consisted of day and night test. The day test required finding five out of eight locations in five hours while the night test consisted of finding three out of five in three hours. During practice, I only passed the day test. I was fearful of the night portion of the course because not only did not want to trip and fall at night but also I had a true fear of venturing out in the dark. During the actual test, I was really nervous and wanted it to be over with because I was tired from walking up and down the hills. Little did I know, my adventure just started. After finding only three locations, I lost my protractor; a crucial tool that is needed to plot a course on a map.

Without my protractor, I seemed to have walked for-ever before I stumbled across a course checkpoint situated in a forest clearing. I was frustrated because I didn't know where I was going and angry with myself for losing my protractor. To my surprise, the clearing was actually a Sergeant Major's safety observation point. He scolded me for mistaking his area as one of the check points. However, when he noticed that I was uneasy he asked me what was my problem. As I explained myself, he told me to move on since I still had a compass. I was infuriated because I knew that without a protractor, I would fail the test.

I reached a real checkpoint and borrowed a protractor from a nice and gorgeous-looking Second Lieutenant. The clock was ticking, however, and I had to hurry and find my points, and forgot about the handsome man. After tripping and falling on logs and brushes over the hills, I could not walk any faster because of my blistered feet. Without finding two other points, I decided to head back to the start/finish point grading tent. It took me by surprise that I still had the energy to run to the grading tent with a few minutes to spare. It was a relief when the graders told me that I made it. As I walked out of the tent, the Sergeant First Class who was in charge of our platoon asked me how I did and with a big grin on my face I gave him two thumbs up. He smiled back at me. When I walked towards him he said, "Cendaña, when you walked out of the tent, I thought you were going to do this (motioning his arms and hands upward to the sky as if he was praising the Lord)." Honestly, I felt like doing what he thought I was going to do, but I did not want to make a big scene. God was really watching over me to allow me to pass even the night land navigation. When all of us came back to our campsite at around 1:30 in the morning, some went right to sleep while others still had energy left to talk about their adventures in the woods. When we all awoke, we found out how we did as a platoon (consisting of forty-four cadets divided into four squads). No one in my squad needed to repeat the test. Consequently, a cadet from Mississippi State University then coined our squad 'Sewer rats: the best land navigators." I was proud to have been a part of that squad. Later, I wondered how my squad would have felt had I failed the test. I was just thankful that the three non-waiverable events, physical fitness, written and practical land navigation, were over and we went on to the situational training exercises.

The Situational Training Exercises or STX brought to my attention the things I took for granted like the simple roof over my head and the comfort of a bed to sleep in. Unlike my basic training as an enlisted soldier, the training staff at NALC stripped me of my "luxurious" sleep tent and sleeping bag.

During Squad STX (consisting of 8 to 12 cadets), teams of people in my squad had the time to put up our two-person tents and we were allowed to use our sleeping bags. So even when it rained, we remained warm. When we conducted the Platoon STX, however, there was no chance for us to put up tents and sleeping bags were not available. We were told that we had to "train as we fight." I remembered sleeping in rain gear and other warm gear in my ruck sack, but the gear was not enough to keep me from shivering. When I pulled my guard duty or night watch, I also noticed that other cadets in my platoon were shivering in their sleep — apparently, I was not the only one that was cold that night. My next few experiences humbled me.

In training like this, we were always moving. We ate when we could as there was no set time to eat our MRE (meal, ready-to-eat). One morning, we were assigned our fighting positions in our security perimeter; our leader told us that we may eat. As I got comfortable in my position, I grabbed my MRE out my sack pocket and I ate as I was lying down on my side. I could not help but notice the ants, spiders and other critters on the ground. I thought it was truly humbling to be eating and sharing space right next to the creatures I felt were a nuisance. I was hilarious that I took notice of those critters and thought, "Hello spider, hello ant."

Due to high activity during the exercise my metabo-lism increased and I constantly ate during STX. The times I felt real lucky was when I would find two beef jerky sticks inside my MRE. It seems like a small thing, but it was nice to have an extra snack to pull out when my stomach began to growl with hunger. My battle buddy was jealous when I got the extra beef jerky and looked at me as if she wanted to bite the snack right out of my hand. When I realized that she was not kidding, I gave her my extra snack. I was very good at giving food away that my platoon noticed me. They also noticed that I continually ate trail mix and granola bars which were my energy source. One time, a cadet from the University of Tennessee with a perfect southern accent, smiled inquisitively at me as I shoved a handful trail mix in my mouth. When it was time for him to be in charge, I asked where he wanted me in the perimeter. He said, "I will put you where you can eat." I laughed out loud. I will never forget that comment.

When graduation came, all of the hard work and sacrifice I made appeared so miniscule. I realized that I only tasted an iota of the sacrifice that our infantrymen have sworn to do. I became conscious and appreciative of their dedication and commitment to the job they willingly signed up for in the Army. When I led my squad on an attack of a bunker, I quickly learned to value human life. When the bullet and other armament simulators were going off, it was very easy to get confused, but we had to keep our composure because our squad relied on each other to stay alive. With this, I encourage friends and family to live each day like it is the last, whenever I have the opportunity.


## CTLT at Ft. Huachuca, Arizona

I was scheduled to attend Cadet Troop Leadership Training (CTLT) right after NALC. As per my request, I was offered to attend CTLT in Wiesbaden, Germany. I thought it was a good opportunity for me to visit my German friends and the cities where I lived while stationed there. The branch training offer, however, was Ordnance and that quickly changed my mind. I wanted to be a Military Intelligence (MI) Officer so I thought it was only fitting to go to Ft. Huachuca because it is the home of the Military Intelligence

Corps. After NALC, however, I was weary and all I wanted to do was go home.

When I and my fellow cadets from Duke University, Florida State University and the University of Puerto Rico arrived at the Sierra Vista Airport in civilian clothes, my sponsor named First Lieutenant Debbie DeRienzo yelled my first name. It really surprised me that she was able to pick me out of the crowd despite the presence of another Asian cadet. We then headed to Ft. Huachuca in my sponsor's car and she dropped me off at the hotel. I was so thankful that I didn't have a roommate since I had been accustomed to living on my own in college. I thought I was spoiled when I noticed that my hotel room was bigger than my one-bedroom apartment. I also thought I was treated well as a Sergeant, but being a cadet was even better. After marveling at how fortunate I was, I changed into my uniform because I had to attend a training meeting with the company that day.

During the meeting, my ears were ringing and I had a splitting headache. I managed to keep my composure because I was facing the company staff and sitting next to Debbie. Despite the pain, I wanted to appear disciplined. When my orientation was over, Debbie dropped me off at the hotel again to get some rest and be ready for the next day.

The next three weeks of training was like a free vacation. My fellow cadets and I hiked up a mountain one Saturday and drove to Nogales, Mexico one Sunday. On another Saturday, my sponsor took me to Tombstone (where the movie 'Tombstone' was filmed).

The numerous instructions I obtained from the training were invaluable to me and my military career. I was so glad I had the opportunity to attend CTLT. Of all my gains though, the greatest I would say was my friendship with Debbie and her husband Mike. They are one of a kind people who, as a couple, devoted their lives to God's service. Debbie led praise and worship at various soldier church services as she was gifted in musical instruments while Mike, who is also an officer in the Army, was studying to become a pastor.

## Back to Iowa

At last training was over, but life did not stop there for me. I contemplated taking graduate courses at the University of Iowa while finishing ROTC program requirements. Yet, I planned to work instead, since I would be back on active duty upon commissioning in December. I hunted for jobs in the civilian world to see how I would fair.

A preliminary interview at General Nutrition Center for a store manager position didn't look promising. The first interviewer was shaking her head while she looked over my resume. I had no retail experience except for my McDonald's job at age 18 let alone retail management. Though I felt I did not have the chance, I prayed that I would be given an interview with the Regional Sales Director. My prayer was granted. During the interview, I left no question unanswered. In addition, instead of having the interviewer ask me what I was made of, I asked him what type of person he wanted to have for the job. Once he explained, I then told him the types of job I was in charge of in the Army in line with the position they have opened. It took him two days to release his decision as there were other applicants still to be interviewed after our meeting. Simply put, I got the job. I managed the store for almost four months until I was commissioned as a Second Lieutenant on the third week of December with orders to South Korea, my first duty station as an officer.

Of the 17 Army officer branches or jobs, the Cadet Accessions Board granted me my first choice of the Military Intelligence branch. I was extremely elated when I was first told about it; it was a dream come true. I thought that there was no other branch that fit as well with my education, language skills, and personality. I thanked and praised God for the opportunity.

## Gold Bar Recruiting at the University of Iowa

As I waited to attend the Officer Basic Course at Ft. Huachuca, Arizona, I had the privilege of working at the Army ROTC at the University of Iowa for over four months. One of the greatest opportunities I had there was working under one of the most talented and respected officers named Captain Stacy Seaworth who remains a mentor to me today. She ensured that I and a fellow Lieutenant, Richard Anderson, were coached and mentored about how to be an Army officer. It was also a privilege to have worked with the ROTC secretary Ms. Sharyl Grimm. She took care of me in my administrative needs as a cadet and again as a lieutenant.

Richard and I went to various colleges within and outside of the University of Iowa to advertise the Army. We would set up booths to encourage students to sign up for the Army ROTC scholarship program and we would contact vendors to order custom made complimentary items for the ROTC program. Also, I had fun in having a chance to apply my arts and crafts skills in designing bulletin boards in the ROTC building and for the University of Iowa campus. My time as a gold bar recruiter gave me an appreciation for what I went through as a cadet and recruiting allowed me to interact with the next generation of Army soldiers.

Michelle Fernandez Cendaña

# Chapter 10

## Officer Basic Course: Forgiveness and Heartbrokenness

*"Be kind and compassionate to one another, forgiving each other, just as in Christ God forgave you." Ephesians 4:32*

<u>Officer Basic Course</u>

I left Iowa City two days after our dining out. My car was packed with my army gear and other personal belongings that I thought were necessary for my four and half months of training at Ft. Huachuca. I was given five days to complete my travel. With a road atlas on hand and enough music to listen to, I embarked on a three and half day journey to Arizona. For safety reasons, I drove less than 400 miles a day. I drove during the day and checked in at night in cheap hotels near my 400 miles mark each day. This was my first three-day road trip in the US alone.

The trip showed me the vastness of the US while only driving through seven states: Iowa, Missouri, Kansas, Oklahoma, Texas, New Mexico and Arizona. I enjoyed my time driving, daydreaming, singing and talking with the Lord. At rest stops, I met people of various backgrounds and carried on short conversations with them. A number of them gave me their contact information and I gave them my e-mail address in return.

Three and a half days passed in a blink of an eye and my drive from Iowa to Arizona was completed. I reported to the company in charge of our training needs for administrative in-processing. Since I was not in uniform, I was told to put on my uniform and be present for further in-processing in the afternoon. Later, I met other new officer trainees who showed up at Fort Huachuca earlier than the commencement of the class. We were put on detail and conducted tasks that needed to be done in the office.

A few days later, all expected officer trainees on active duty, reserves and the National Guard in our class arrived. Our TAC (Tactical) officer brought us all together in a huge room and our battalion commander and command sergeant major briefed us on our training environment and the do's and dont's while undergoing training. Further, we were told of the things that were expected of us as trainees and as officers in the United States Army. Afterwards, our TAC officer separated us into groups and ensured that the Americans sponsored the international students in our class.

In the classroom, I learned how different we were from each other, but that we had one common goal, which was to graduate from Officer Basic Course. There was a moment when I was extremely impressed in knowing that I was in the same class with two US diplomats, a doctorate student at Oxford University and a law student. Although at first I was intimidated in knowing that brilliant people surrounded me, I counted myself blessed to be among them.

As days went by and we came to know more of each other in and out of the classroom, we became very close. A few of us hosted parties in their apartment complexes for everyone to attend. I will never forget all the fond memories we created with one another. We found ourselves barbecuing, golfing, eating breakfast at local restaurants on weekends and sightseeing. In the classroom, we worked as a team and we helped each other out. It was amazing how we made our time at Fort Huachuca so wonderful and memorable.

## Asking for Forgiveness

In the midst of having a great time learning and doing all other activities, a pleasant surprise came along. One evening while studying for an exam, my mom randomly called me on my cell phone. She was crying like I had never heard her cry before asking me for forgiveness for all she did to me in the past. She explained she didn't understand why she treated me the way she did. My emotions overwhelmed me that I was silently crying while listening to all she was saying and the God of compassion reached out to me. Wholeheartedly, I said, "What happened before has passed; we need to move on and look forward to a better relationship."

Truthfully, I forgave her many years before that time for my sake without her asking for forgiveness. Although it took me a while to realize, I believed in forgiving others so that I was able to live in peace and harmony. I never dreamed of the time that she would ask me for forgiveness, but I prayed a countless times with God that He would touch her heart and that she would come to know Christ as her Lord and Savior. God revealed how much He cared about me because He forgave me first. He enabled me to forgive the person whom I thought I could not forgive.


Heartbrokenness

Before I graduated from the University of Iowa, I fell in love with a classmate of mine. Although he was one year behind me, we stayed in contact while I attended Officer Basic Course (OBC). We had some troubled times with the distance apart from each other, but I enjoyed talking with him and I longed for him to visit me. Ironically, the thing that I longed for the most in my heart, broke my heart.

After he finished his ROTC program and his training at Ft. Lewis, he flew out to see me on a Thursday evening. I thought that after not seeing him for a few months, my feelings for him had dissipated but I was wrong; I was still much in love with him.

He had only two days to spend with me since I was in class during the week. Therefore, we rushed everywhere to see awesome canyons and other views in the towns of Sierra

Vista, Bisbee, Nogales, Mexico and Tombstone. Oddly, we avoided talking about the issues we were having and only focused on enjoying the moment together.

The night before he flew back to Iowa, I felt unsettled about not talking about where our relationship was going to go in the future. I felt that he was drawing away because there might be someone else attracting his attention. Although I didn't want to bring up the past, I felt the need to ask him to tell me the truth. He told me that my intuition was correct, although hearing him say it literally torn me apart inside. I never felt so small in my life until that moment and I felt sick to my stomach I wanted to throw up.

We argued over the subtleties of the situation, but inside I felt helpless and all I could do was cry hard and loud. Then, he dropped the bomb and said "Michelle, I couldn't imagine myself being married to you." I could not believe what I just heard and I couldn't shake it off. I forced him to tell me why and convinced him that I could handle it, though I didn't want to hear it from him. Off the cuff, he said "I don't like the way you laugh, you're uptight and a goody-two-shoes."

My thoughts were racing. I couldn't believe the man I thought I was going to marry just told me he couldn't imagine himself being married to me and one of his reasons was because he didn't like what was naturally a part of me. I knew his reasons were superficial but I responded and said, "No one can take my laughter away from me except God Himself." I explained to him my laughter was nearly lost, but God revived it and reminded him of my life story. He felt horrible and didn't know what to do so I sent him to the bathroom to get a wet towel to sooth my swollen eyes.

The next day we awoke, I didn't want to go to church for my eyes showed that I cried the night before, but I promised Andrea, my best friend at OBC, and her boyfriend that we would go to church together. Pretending like things were normal, I didn't tell Andrea right away what had happened. We went through the motions at church and ate lunch with my friends afterwards. Then, we went back to billeting to pick up his belongings and on we drove to the airport.

The hour and half drive to the airport seemed forever especially because I didn't want to talk at all. He tried extremely hard to get me to talk with him while he was driving. Whether it was fortunate or unfortunate, I was not a hard person to make amends with so even if my mind forbade me to speak, my heart reached out in love even though I knew that I may just have been fooled. When we got to the airport, I didn't just drop him off at the curb; I thought it was appropriate for me to see him off. My heart was hoping in the hope of hopes that we would get back together one day while my mind was vowing to never speak with him again.

I drove back to Sierra Vista from the airport alone, lonely, and distraught. The drive back home was an hour and half, and it gave me plenty of time to reflect on both my current pain and on a previous relationship in which I had emotionally hurt someone as well. I told a previous boyfriend that I did not want to see him simply because he directed obscenities towards me. Even after begging for forgiveness, I was pretty much unforgiving after he broke my simply rules. My current incident prompted me to call him to apologize about everything. I looked him up on the Army Knowledge Online directory and hesitantly dialed his number. It was such a relief, when I heard him say, "It's okay Michelle, my girlfriend and I now have a son." The conversation served as a good closure for me, and gave me a new perspective on how to move on with my life.

Monday came and I told Andrea about what happened. She tried to comfort me by saying that it was his loss but in not so nice terms. I understood what she was trying to tell me, but deep in my heart I asked that if it was his loss and not mine then why didn't he seem to be hurt while I was crying over it. These were the times when I started to think about my assignment to Korea as God's grace. I questioned God why He was sending me to Korea; I learned why at that time. I didn't doubt that God had His plan which I couldn't see. At this point, all I wanted to do was to go to a faraway place.

It was tough to go on every day, but with God's mercy, I survived. My sister and my niece came to visit me for 10 days while I was in transition out of Ft. Huachuca. There visit helped ease my suffering. It was as if my world just shattered before my eyes and I needed another time and space for me to deal with my broken heart. The Lord had sent me to the perfect place — Korea.

# Chapter 11

## Assignment to South Korea:
## Self-Acceptance and Recovery

*"He heals the brokenhearted, binding up their wounds."*
*Psalm 147:3*

My sister, my niece and I drove a rental car early in the morning from Sierra Vista to the airport to catch our flights. They were going back to San Diego while I was going to South Korea for the first time. Nevertheless, at that moment, I'd been so preoccupied with my own pain I thought it was better to be far away from family than for them to see me hurting.

### Arrival in the 'Land of the Morning Calm'

I arrived at the Incheon International Airport with the sun already set so I couldn't really see the beauty of the 'Land of the Morning Calm' known as South Korea. For nearly an hour, I, along with other soldiers, waited at the United Services Organization lounge for our ride to register and in-process at Yongsan Garrison located in the heart of Seoul. Despite the fact that I couldn't see much and I was jetlagged, the night view of Seoul was beautiful. After a briefing, we settled into our hotel rooms at the Dragon Hill Lodge located on the military post.

The next day, I was awake by three or four and couldn't fall back to sleep. I learned later that the others had the same experience. We went to breakfast and reported for further in-processing. After an all-morning long briefing, we were told that our sponsors would meet us upon our arrival at our duty location. They gave us our bus tickets, one for each of us and one for our luggage. Finally, we left the military post and were on our journey to our new duty station.

The drive from Seoul to Anjung-ri was about an hour and I was excited to see the countryside of Korea so I made sure I was awake no matter how tired I was. I couldn't help, but think about how prosperous a country Korea was considering that it was war-torn just over 50 years ago. I asked myself if the Philippines would somehow improve its economy and be as prosperous as Korea. As we continued to travel, I stood in awe how God brought me to another place I never imagined I would visit.

I arrived at Camp Humphreys bus station in Anjung-ri and was picked up by a first lieutenant in his own car. He brought me to the company area to meet with the leadership and to sign-in. Then, he took me to the hotel on post so I could settle in for the next few days of in-processing. The hotel was fully booked so I checked-in to a hotel just outside the post; I stayed there until a room in the single officer's quarters on-post became available. Staying off post was an opportunity for me to be immersed in the Korean language, life and culture immediately.

My first few days in Korea were very interesting. Many Koreans I encountered thought I was Korean. They started speaking Korean with me, but with a smile on my face and a respectful gesture, I told them in English that I didn't speak Korean. There was one I encountered, however, who was adamant about my national origin who said to me, "Your mother or your father must be Korean." In knowing that I wouldn't be able to convince her otherwise, I said, "Maybe, you're right," and bowed my head, a sign of respect in Korea.

The in-processing within the organization and on post took less than a week. At first, I was extremely disoriented, but I was thankful that I quickly became friends with fellow lieutenants in our organization that helped me immensely. Nikko, Antonio, Josh and Young, all were lieutenants at the time, ensured that I was well taken care of. However, Nikko and Antonio became my best buddies and were the first ones to introduce me to Korean food and culture. Moreover my two buddies, also pointed out the shady bars and clubs that many of my soldiers frequented when they were off duty.

I had no idea that my friend Demechel "Mechel" Robinson whom I met at NALC was in the hotel I stayed in also. One evening, I was on my way out to meet with Nikko for dinner and the elevator opened. When I looked at who was coming out of it, I saw a familiar face and when Mechel looked at me we started screaming and hugging each other. The receptionist laughed at us. Mechel then joined me and Nikko for dinner. Almost instantly, we all had common ground and interests, because we all had Filipino ancestry.

## Meeting missionaries at the Camp Humphreys Protestant Church

Mechel and I went to a church service on post the first Sunday of our arrival to Korea. We didn't talk about what we were going to wear so we were surprised to see each other on the lobby wearing nearly the same outfit: black dress suit with a white shirt underneath. We could be twins. At church, the pastor asked new comers to go up front to introduce ourselves. Mechel introduced herself first and I went second. We both had the congregation laughing especially with the way we introduced ourselves as Filipinos.

After the service, people shook our hands and wel-comed us into the church community. Then, a couple approached us and introduced themselves to us. As we conversed, they told us that they were missionaries in the Philippines in the 70's. They were Dennis and Betty Ortman who invited us to check out the Hospitality House located just outside the post.

## The Hospitality House

The Hospitality House catered to the Christian Fellowship needs of soldiers and their families. It was sponsored by Cadence Ministries International. The house became a refuge for many soldiers. We conducted Bible studies, partook in home-cooked meals weekly, took part in cultural tours, and went to amusement parks. Throughout my two-year tour in Korea, the hospitality house became my home away from home; the missionaries were like our parents and all members became each other's family. Like a family, we could always count on one another.

As I regularly attended Bible studies, I came to know Dennis and Betty. They were the ones whom the Lord sent for me to start healing my broken heart. They both saw how wrecked I was and were always listening to me and praying with and for me. I will never forget how much time they spent with me to help me recover from heartbrokenness and to cope with my challenges at work. Indeed, they treated me like one of their daughters.

## At work

Arriving fresh from Ft. Huachuca from the Military Intelligence School, my battalion commander assigned me as the platoon leader for the Network Operation Center. Before I signed into the unit, he was under the false impression that I was a Signal or Communications Officer. When he realized during my initial orientation that I was not a Signal Officer but an MI Officer, he slated me to work as the Assistant S-3, Plans and Training. Working there was a great experience not only in learning about how a battalion operates, but also it was there that I learned genuine service to my superior despite the fact that I disliked him at first. At that time, I applied the Bible study lessons I learned at the Hospitality House about the topic of "Submission" as mentioned in Ephesians 6:5-8 which states, *"Slaves, obey*

*your earthly masters with respect and fear, and with*
*sincerity of heart, just as you would obey Christ. Obey them*
*not only to win their favor when their eye is on you, but like*
*slaves of Christ, doing the will of God from your heart. Serve*
*wholeheartedly, as if you were serving the Lord, not men,*
*because you know that the Lord will reward everyone for*
*whatever good he does, whether he is slave or free."*

The second week of my arrival at Camp Humphreys,
I received my initial counseling with our Battalion
Commander, Lieutenant Colonel Robert Harms. He briefed
me of the battalion's mission and operations, his expecta-
tions of me and on the soldiers' life in Korea. For that short
session, he learned a little bit about me and he said, "Don't
allow anyone to change you." I walked out of his office
knowing he was an awesome commander.

Soon after my new job, I developed my routine. I
stayed at work quite late countless times. It was true that we
had a lot of work that needed get done in the office almost
daily, but I worked until I was tired just to avoid thinking
and rethinking about my failed relationship. I coped with my
challenges by working until late evening. My immediate
supervisor, CPT Keith Cockrell, tried to send me home
around six in the evening every single work day, but I
always managed to stay behind in the office. One evening,
CPT Cockrell, on his way out of the office, asked me why I
was staying at work late all the time. When I told him that I
was trying to avoid thinking too much about my situation, he
sat behind the desk that was directly across from mine to
listen and speak with me.

After my long and tedious explanation, he said,
"Kick his @!# to the curb; I better not meet this guy." Like
a big brother, he told me to take care of myself and gave me
advice on how to cope and start living my life. He allowed
me to stay in the office late, but told me that I should take a
break and do something fun aside from working. With my
plan on extending my one-year tour to two years, he said, "I
hope that you are doing this for you. Take the time to know

---

yourself." Little by little, the Lord began to heal my heart, mind and soul.

After working as an Assistant S-3 for four and a half months, I became a company executive officer working for Captain Shawn East and alongside First Sergeant Krista Munyon. Both of them were awesome leaders in my eyes. They set an example for me and for the soldiers to emulate. Captain East was a leader who gave me needed guidance and the time to execute tasks or missions. The most important thing I appreciated about him was the fact that he trusted that I would accomplish given tasks without his need to constantly check on me. In like manner, First Sergeant Munyon trusted her subordinate Non-Commissioned Officers and soldiers to do what was right for their good and the company's. I worked with both of them for six months until they were replaced by Captain Cockrell and First Sergeant Young.

## Believing and seeing God's miracles

My additional duties as an executive officer were the dining facility; supply operations; weapons room; nuclear, biological and chemical room; motor pool officer; and perimeter defense force (PDF) platoon leader. Among these duties, the most time-consuming jobs were the dining facility and PDF. I prayed hard for God's miracle when I found out a month after I took over the dining facility that we overspent $20,000. My focus had been divided between the dining facility and PDF as we constantly had civilian demonstrations just outside the post. I knew full well that I was going in different directions and some areas of my duties were suffering from my lack of attention. There was no way I could do it alone so I was on my knees praying fervently for guidance, wisdom, courage and strength. He was faithful to carry me through all my challenges.

The Lord reversed our financial situation in the dining facility without us doing anything illegal or immoral. In addition, we manned our sector's towers in response to civilian demonstrations without any incident. Our company underwent several Department of the Army level inspections and evaluations with commendable results. Soldiers within our sphere of influence gave their best in what they did daily. I couldn't think of any other reason how or why the company performed the way it did had it not been for God's miracles of provision.

## Revisiting the Philippines

Since I had gone home to Hawaii in June 2004, I decided to spend Christmas 2004 and New Year's in the Philippines. At that time, I convinced myself that it was important for me to know more about my biological mother as part of the process in knowing myself. While traveling from Manila to Pangasinan with my cousins and uncles, I asked questions about my mother. My uncle, Ching, whom my mom followed in the birth order told me that my mother was a good person, except for the fact that she prioritized having fun with friends while in college. I nearly laughed when my uncle mentioned that my mother was normal in her childhood and teenage years. Further, my uncle told me that they never knew she was pregnant until she gave birth.

Uncle Ching continued to explain that perhaps the reason why my mother died giving birth to me was that she lacked prenatal care; she hid her pregnancy well. Had she not hid it her life story may have been different according to my uncle. Uncle Ching and my mother roomed together while in college in Manila. He told me further that after my mother transferred to another school from Manila to Pangasinan, he never really knew what had happened to my mother until after she had given birth and died.

At around midnight, we arrived at my grandmother's house in Pangasinan. As we pulled in to her garage, I was expecting my grandmother to come out of her house to meet me. A few minutes later, my Uncle Wilson came out and asked if we were going straight to the hospital. Uncle Ching and I were in shock when we were told that my grandmother was in the hospital; I cried. Little did I know, Grandma had a stroke, but they spared me the news until I arrived in Pangasinan.

The next day we went to the hospital and saw Grandma who, by the grace of God, was doing fine. It was four days before Christmas and my prayer was that we wouldn't spend Christmas in the hospital. The Lord was merciful that Grandma was released on the 24th of December and I remembered the occasion as God's answer to my prayer. Grandma was doing much better and was undergoing physical therapy at home. With my grandma's medical condition, I realized I couldn't ask her about my mother, but the Lord provided my grandmother's younger sister Nana (Pangasinan term for aunt) Juana to answer my questions.

Nana Juana explained to me that the night my mother was going to give birth to me, my mother simply asked my grandparents to take her to the hospital because she had a stomachache. They took her to Pangasinan Medical Hospital and as soon as they arrived, according to Nana Juana, they asked if my mother was pregnant. Since my grandparents didn't know that she was, they said, "She can't be pregnant because she is not married." They then injected my mother with a painkiller to ease her stomach pains.

A few minutes later, my mother told my grandparents that she needed to use the bathroom. When they sat her down in the toilet, she said in a Filipino dialect, "Nanay, I am going to give birth." They rushed her to the delivery room. Nana Juana didn't tell me whether or not my mother delivered normal or Caesarian section, but that she bled too much and that it was unstoppable. I couldn't comprehend how I survived the delivery and she didn't. All I know now is that I experienced God's miracle in my own life.

This trip to the Philippines gave me an appreciation for my biological mother like never before. I couldn't help, but get emotional when I heard about her story; the sacrifice that she went through for me. I understand that I was a product of her disobedience of God's laws, but praise the Lord that I was not a mistake and that He fearfully and wonderfully made me.

## Public singing opportunities

Upon my return to Korea from my trip to the Philippines, I, along with my best friend Christina Fanitizi and a soldier from our organization named Specialist Carpenter were selected to compete in the US Army's Stars of Tomorrow at Fort Belvoir, Virginia. I didn't expect to be deeply involved in singing competitions in our community's talent shows. As the Lord continued to heal me, He was giving me opportunities to showcase the talent He gave me. Bill and Kathy Ladd who were the Hospitality House's missionaries at the time encouraged me to perform for God's glory. The fact that I was an entertainer and participated in singing competitions surprised my soldiers because prior they only knew me as a quiet and shy officer.

We were in Virginia for five days for the competition, which was an awesome exposure to the Army entertainment world. The competition opened my eyes showing me that the Army had extremely talented individuals who are not shy to share it. Further, the competition became an opportunity for me to see the Isgrigs again after five years. The Isgrigs were surprised and wondered what had happened to me to make me sing in public since they never really saw or heard me participate in any singing competitions in Germany. Nonetheless, they supported me and were proud of my accomplishments.

I didn't win the Stars of Tomorrow competition however I was grateful to have given my best and to have been able to perform in front of active voters of the Grammy Awards. Not winning in the competition didn't stop me from pursuing my audition for the 2005 US Army Soldier Show (an entertainment production performed in the US and overseas military bases). I was selected as one of the 25 finalists to be cast members of the Soldier Show, but our leadership was unable to let me go. There was so much drama that arose around the issue of my participation in the competition that I remembered my impassioned prayer to God that if it was not His will that I would be able to graciously accept it.

For quite some time, I was sad that the opportunity was passing me by. But, the Lord is really awesome in that He gave me a chance to improve my stage presence through the help of an entertainment director named Mr. John Antes who also helped me get into the final cut of the Soldier Show. Mr. Antes called me one early morning to tell me that since I wasn't let go to join the Soldier Show, he suggested that I keep at what I started. He asked, "Have you thought of modeling?" I laughed at him thinking that he was playing around. Then he said, "I am not kidding. Please don't think I am being disrespectful, but you have a beautiful face and a nice body. I want you to walk the runway so you can conquer the stage whenever you sing." I struggled with the idea of modeling again because early in life I decided against it because I thought it was not what God wanted me do. However, after talking with my long-term mentor in Christ, she put the idea into perspective in such a way that I agreed to model.

At this point in my Korean tour, we had Denny and Jeannie Roth as the Hospitality House's missionaries. They came into my life when there was that little spark of hope in my heart and I completely recovered from my relationship heartaches. Denny and Jeannie made me believe in myself, showed me that I could do what I wanted to do and they put my desire to model in perspective. With the encouragement of Denny and Jeannie and my big sister Eunhee, who was my style guru while in Korea, I participated in fashion shows.

I never would have thought a 25-meter runway could be intimidating. My first catwalk was horrible during our rehearsal. The organizer/trainer for the event told Mr. Antes that I needed a lot of work; I wasn't surprised. Mr. Antes never gave up on me and he kept on training me. I worked hard, placed myself on a strict diet and sacrificed a lot of my time traveling for rehearsals and for the actual fashion shows. In the end, I realized Mr. Antes was correct. After my runway experiences, I felt more confident performing on stage.

## Mom's passing

Captain Cockrell was on leave and I was the acting company commander when an American Red Cross message came. First Sergeant Roberts called me up on my cell phone stating that there was a Red Cross message and I needed to come into the office. As soon as I walked into her office, she sat me down and handed a clip board with a sheet of paper and said, "It's for you." After reading the message that mom was in critical condition, I sat there for a moment and didn't know what to think or say. The first sergeant asked me what I was going to do. I flew home the next day.

My sister picked me up at Kahului Airport and we drove straight to the hospital. My first sight of Mom made me emotional, but I kept my composure. Mom looked really haggard but she found the strength to say something nice to me. She said in a Filipino dialect, "Michelle, you've become very beautiful." Everyone in the room laughed insinuating that Mom must have wanted something from me because of what she said.

On the 10th day I was home, Mom was brought to the Intensive Care Unit (ICU) again. This time, the nurse told us that Mom was dying. One of Mom's sisters quickly flew in from Honolulu and all of Mom's siblings who were not at work barged into the hospital. For a while, I was in the ICU and feeling physically weak from crying and praying so hard for strength and courage to lead Mom to Christ. I asked God why I was so bold in leading others to Jesus, but I couldn't do it for Mom.

Finally, the Lord gave me everything I needed to walk over to Mom's side. I took her hand and asked if she could hear me. She couldn't talk, but she responded to me. I said, "Mom, if you believe in your heart what I am going to say, you don't have to talk to repeat it, just say it to the Lord. Lord, I repent for all my sins. Come into my life as my Lord and Savior, in Jesus name, Amen!" I knew that Mom received Christ at that moment and was guaranteed the everlasting life. Mom died four days after she received Christ in her life.

Back to Korea

As I was returning to Korea, I was wishing and hoping that Mom had accepted Christ years before her health degraded so she would have lived in God's abundant love, grace and mercy. Also, I thought about Mom's dream which became my dream for her. She once told me that she wanted to visit the Pyramids of Egypt. I never told her about my thoughts, but I planned to take her to Egypt. The dream never came to fruition and I wished that at least I told her of my plan.

It took a while for things to get back to normal, but I realized that I wasn't alone in the battle and I needed to keep on going and believing that things would be better. My assignment to Korea was God-ordained. He used all of my experiences there to make me realize that He loves me so much He wants me to be complete. If my assessment is right, the Lord didn't allow for me to be part of the 2005 Soldier Show so that I could be with Mom in her last days.

Michelle Fernandez Cendaña

# Chapter 12

## Deployment to Iraq: God's Vision and Provision

*"For I know the plans I have for you," declares the Lord, "plans to prosper you and not to harm you, plans to give you hope and a future." Jeremiah 29:11*

After serving in South Korea for two years, I requested to be reassigned to Germany. I returned to the Darmstadt military community with much excitement because it was familiar to me but was also apprehensive because I was training for deployment. The organization I was assigned to had left for Iraq a month before I arrived in Germany. It took a month and half for me to complete in-processing and training before I found myself in the desert.

Deployment to Iraq

What is it like to be deployed in a war zone? I have been on active duty for 11 years and this was my first deployment. I was fearful of being in a war zone. I did not know what to expect and my apprehensiveness clouded my thoughts. "Will I make it back alive?" was the first question I had in mind. Prayerfully trying to be optimistic, I embedded in my mind the statement, "By the grace of God, I will make it back alive and unscathed."

I vividly remember how challenging the first two weeks were for me in Kuwait and in Iraq. Outside, it was very dusty and I could barely breathe and found myself hyperventilating a lot due to the environment and combat stress. Easily, I put in 14-hour to 16-hour days, depending on missions; I didn't and couldn't take my job lightly. As days passed, I became more confident and competent in my job and I appreciated the leaders I worked for such as Lieutenant Colonel Derek Orndorff and Major Eric Derynioski and the soldiers I worked with like Specialist Rose Abido.


## Spiritual Upheaval

I would be lying to myself if I don't admit that I had my spiritual mountains and valleys while there in the desert. Part of me wished that I were anywhere but there. Who wanted to be deployed anyway? My loved ones feared for me, my father blamed himself for my being in Iraq and my grandmother, for her health's sake, didn't even know I was there. I went to a few American bases in Iraq on convoys and on aircraft and I will tell you that I fervently prayed out of fear. Adrenaline rushed through the very core of my being the night before any mission, which resulted in groggy feelings when I awoke. Tired of my seemingly faithless thoughts and feelings, I ended up asking myself, "How much faith do I have in Christ and how much of what I do is an act of faith?" Through questions like that I began to know what not owning my life means and if it's my time to die then there's nothing I could do about it. At least, I'll be with the Lord which is the ultimate goal of being here on earth.

Undoubtedly, the Lord had a purpose and a vision for my deployment. With my struggles, I was reminded of God's love and His words particularly in Jeremiah 29:11 which was quoted to me by Chaplain Byrd before I left Korea : *"For I know the plans I have for you, plans to prosper you and not to harm you, plans to give you hope and a future."*

While in Iraq, the Lord provided all of my spiritual needs. We had regular church services every Sunday and I was one of the Praise and Worship team members. I also attended a small Bible study group led by Chaplain Florio Pierre. Coincidentally in the Bible study group, I met Chief Warrant Officer Perry Nibbelink who just happened to also be a member of the World Harvest International Christian Church. It was a blessing to have had Bible study sessions to break the monotony of my work. Lastly, I found it interesting to have studied with an Iraqi Muslim who converted to Christianity because of an American Chaplain influence in her life.

I made true friends with a number of people I encountered in Baghdad. One of them was my roommate, a Marine Lawyer (Captain), Andie. She was a source of never-ending encouragement and legal advice. Then there was Sergeant First Class Luis Colon. He was my battle buddy who was full of sense of humor and grace in dancing; he taught me steps for my song entry to a Talent Show in Iraq. I had other battle buddies like Captain Katie Diefenbach, Captain Tracy Tawiah, Captain Jennifer Glasscock and Captain Stacy Osborn who made my tour in Iraq bearable.

Our battalion's convoy team, particularly the ones in Baghdad, became an intricate part of my personal and military life. I cared so much for them it felt like they were my brothers. I will always cherish the times when I went on convoys with them and knew that my life was safe in their hands for they were committed to the job that they did daily. Also, for the times that no Chaplain was around, they asked me to pray with them. I appreciated their trust in the God I serve who deserves all honor, praise and glory.

How awesome it was to be a part of an organization that deployed over 3,000 soldiers and all came back alive. I know that it was an act of God that we all left Iraq to be reunited with our families.

Through my deployment, the Lord allowed me to recognize that the most important aspects of my life are my relationships with Christ, and my family and friends.

# Chapter 13

## God's Awesome Love, Grace and Mercy

*"Before I formed you in the womb I knew you, before you were born I set you apart; I appointed you as a prophet to the nations." Jeremiah 1:5*

We may go through things in our lives that are hurtful which throws our focus away from God. However, I am convinced that those things happen so that God could bring us to another plateau of our faith. We are, but humans that, at times, react to tribulations with rage. Yet, I hope and pray that we never forget to repent, to be thankful and to draw joy from the God who never changes (Hebrews 13:8 says, *"Jesus Christ is the same yesterday and today and forever"*) when our situations change in a way we could not fathom.

More than once, I asked the Lord to show me why I had to endure hardships throughout my life. At the Lord's appointed time, He revealed to me that without my humbling experiences I would not be the woman I am today. The Lord, with His infinite wisdom, perfectly orchestrated the sequence of events in my life for me to experience His awesome love, grace and mercy.

It says in James 5:11, *"As you know, we consider blessed those who have persevered. You have heard of Job's perseverance and have seen what the Lord finally brought about. The Lord is full of compassion and mercy."* May you remember this passage of the Bible from Zephaniah 3:17, *"The Lord your God is with you, he is mighty to save. He will take great delight in you, he will quiet you with his love, he will rejoice over you with singing."*

In no less than wonderful and powerful ways, I pray in the matchless name of Jesus that you may taste and see the goodness of the Lord in your life.